LIGHTS OF CONSCIOUSNESS

A Sufi View of Science and Spirituality

Adnan Al Adnani

Publisher: Quintessence Publishing
ISBN: 978-0-620-66555-1
Typeset by: Quintessence Publishing
Cover design by: Quintessence Publishing
Printed by: www.qpublish.com
© Quintessence Publishing

All rights reserved. Except for brief quotations in critical articles or reviews, no part of this book may be reproduced in any manner without prior written permission from Quintessence Publishing.

Table of Contents

Dedication	vii
Foreword	ix
Acknowledgments	xiii
Preface	1
Introduction	3
Who Am I?	3
1 - The Fabric of Reality	15
Foundation	16
A Universal Science	18
Manifest Hierarchy	23
2 - The View of Origins	33
Beginnings	33
A Brief History of Time	37
Invariance	44
Imagination	47
3 - The View of Light	51
A New World	52
Quantum Age	54
Conscious Light	56
4 - The View of Time and Space	59
Sacred Geometry	59
Mindscapes	63
Orientations	67
5 - The View of Matter and Energy	71
Primal Uncertainty	71
Field Transformations	77
Formations	80

Perceptual Patterns	83
6 - The View of Quanta	**87**
Matter Myth	87
Confirmations	90
Implicate Wholeness	93
Transcendence	96
7 - The View of Mind	**99**
Magic of Mathematics	99
Incompleteness	104
Metaphysical Symbolism	106
Sacred Projections	108
8 - The View of the Biosphere	**111**
Bio Emergence	111
Thinking Machine	112
The Making of Memory	115
Self-Organization	117
Emergence	118
Dreamscapes	119
Culturescapes	122
Uniscape	125
9 - The View of Philosophy	**129**
The Quest for Meaning	129
Noumenon	133
Non-duality	139
Gnostic *Hikma*	142
10 - The View of Self	**149**
Basic Sketch	150
Meeting the Mark	152
A Sufi Map	155
Molecular Base	160

Human Drives	160
Revelation	162
Cosmological Sketch	163
Reflective Mystery	166
Origins	167
Stages	170
Current View	173
11 - The View of the Imaginal	**179**
Mundus Imaginalis	180
Divine Patterning	183
Finding the Unseen	184
The Station of No Station	186
Eternity and Time	188
Bewilderment	189
12 - The View of Love	**191**
Alchemy	193
13 - *Alma Encantar*	**197**
Enduring the Tides of Time	197
To Be	197
Jahanara	197
Oneness	198
Glossary	**199**
About the Author	**211**

Dedication

To Shaykh Fadhlallah Haeri, whose light helped me see my own shadows.

Hast thou not regarded thy Lord, how He has stretched out the shadow? Had He willed, He would have made it still. Then We appointed the sun, to be a guide to it.
— *Qur'an 25.45*

Foreword

The greatest anomaly within the human mind is the sense of Being. It is not rooted in time and space, nor in causality, nor in any other form of confirmatory experience or knowledge. Every statement we can make of it or about it is simply an assertion- or its mirror image, denial. It can be an assertion that is often rooted in philosophy; in metaphysics; in religion; in aesthetics; in culture- but it is nevertheless an assertion. Denial on the other hand makes its own assertions of precision and exactitude by situating its claims within the perspectives of science and logic. But fundamentally, denial is no different from assertion- it is merely its mirror opposite. Both try to 'concretise' the presence- or absence- of Being in the human being's perception. Both succeed in structuring a scaffolding of comprehension inside which individual and social lives can be built. And both fail in bringing Being into a comprehensive admixture with the human condition. It is this imperceptibility of essence that has baffled human beings from the onset of their consciousness. The unwillingness of human beings to live in perpetual ambiguity brings about another dimension of the paradox- the essence of imperceptibility is its utter unknowability. Therefore, the search for certainty is at best quixotic. So why do human beings persist in making assertions or denials in the light of this cruel fact? Why do we make claims about the void/unknown that preceded our coming into being and the void/unknown that awaits us after we cease our material existence? Why do we embellish it, make remarkable claims about it, gasp in ecstasy or despair about it, or ignore it at our peril? Why indeed?

The answer is really quite simple and baffling at the same time. Existence is made aware of its being by a force, a field, something, which we care to call Consciousness. Whether it is planted, genetically predisposed, or intrinsic is quite immaterial. Its presence is self-evident and its spectrum of vision ranges across infinite fields, but it comes back-always- to its own essence. Necessarily, Consciousness questions itself and in the process seeks to determine its source and its destiny. And necessarily it does not and cannot provide an answer that is final and conclusive to the agency that carries it. It remains in perpetual seeking, knowing- yes, knowing- that its source is elsewhere and its destiny is elsewhere than the agent that is carrying it. So the essence of consciousness is the perpetual awareness of a field in which it is present , but one which it cannot explain or articulate to its carrier. The carrier or agent is left bewildered and flays out unable to definitively separate itself from its consciousness but unable to share in consciousness's own certainty. Just as currents might make a fish aware of its medium, water, so consciousness awakens human beings to the medium of existence into which we are thrust. Beyond that lie only assertions or denials whose only purpose is to create the circumstances where human beings can live out their lives in a modicum of certainty, seeking certainty, or denying the possibility of certainty. The intricacies and complexities that accompany this impossible process of bounding the imperceptible gives rise to the whole panoply of human civilisations, to religions and philosophies. Simplification is not an answer- the basic fallacy of Ockham's Razor. As one simplifies so the target dissolves into a mist, rather than coming into clearer view as the axiom would imply. Neither is rejection, for consciousness would not allow that. The only path that is left is the path that we are offered by reason- a very limited tool to understand the imperceptible- and the possibilities that are provided by our imagination. Their 'reality' is of an altogether different dimension. The combination, which certainly has no definitiveness to it, allows for the possibility of engagement with the simulacrum of imperceptibility. The intensity of this engagement, and its sincerity, gives rise to the possibility of a luminous life between the two voids or unknowns of coming into existence and leaving it. In short, this is the relativisation of Truth into 'truth' and a passage into the possibility of a fulfilling and thrilling spirituality.

Adnan al-Adnani's remarkable essay on Consciousness tackles this matter directly. Prophets, mystics, scientists, philosophers have all participated in the effort to explicate the imperceptible, while knowing the futility of such an effort. Terms such as duality/non-duality; light/shadow; spirit/matter; absolute/contingent; unity/multiplicity are generated to create categories through which we can try to engage with the shadow of imperceptibility, which we sometimes conflate with Truth . In the Light of Consciousness, Adnani brings the perspectives of science into the equation and demonstrates that in spite of its own pretensions, science is merely another agent- albeit a very potent one- in the quest to find or impose certainty on structural ambiguity. In the final analysis, the insights of mystics and quantum scientists, of metaphysicians and prophets, all blend into a universal demand for access to the Truth- while fully conscious of the fact that access to the Truth is a chimerical construct to eternally hide Truth from manifestations of Itself.

--Dr. Ali Allawi, author of The Crisis of Islamic Civilization, The Occupation of Iraq and Faisal I of Iraq

Acknowledgments

I would like to express my gratitude to the many people who saw me through this book; to all those who provided support, discussed, read, wrote, offered comments, and assisted in the editing, proofreading and design.

Above all I want to thank my wife Bara for her initial editorial work, who supported and encouraged me in this journey.

I would like specifically to thank Shaykh Fadhlalla Haeri, Aliya Batul Haeri, Shabnam Dharamsi, Abdullah Maynard, Saleem Andrew McGroarty, Nadia Mason, Marguerite Lake, Sadia Bundgaard. Appreciation to Leyya Kalla at Quintessence Publishing for the diligent work on producing this book, and especially Shafia Mahomed, for helping me in the process of editing and finalising the book.

Last, and not least, I beg forgiveness of all those who have been with me over the course of the years and whose names I have failed to mention.

Preface

Yet none shall receive it, except the steadfast; none shall receive it, except who is of mighty fortune.
—*Qur'an 41.35*

The journey of life manifests as follows: Oblivion (pure consciousness), forgetfulness, disillusionment, longing, love, Oblivion.
 This book itself is a manifestation of this journey.

We shall not cease from exploration, and the end of all our exploring will be to arrive where we started and know the place for the first time.
—*T.S. Eliot*

The contents of this book are not copyrighted. They are not 'mine'. Understanding or misunderstanding, interpreting or misinterpreting, quoting or misquoting, using or misusing, appropriating or misappropriating, may or may not occur.

LIGHTS OF CONSCIOUSNESS

Introduction

Recite: In the Name of thy Lord who created.
—Qur'an 96.1

Who am I? The reflection of the Eternal Light.
What is the world? A wave on the Everlasting Sea.
How could the reflection be cut off from the Light?
How could the wave be separate from the Sea?
Know that this reflection and this wave are that very Light and Sea,
for here duality is impossible, impossible.
Look at the travellers on the Path of Love, how each has a different spiritual state.
The one sees in each atom of the world a Sun radiant and imperishable, Another directly witnesses in the mirror of existence the beauty of the hidden archetypes, and a third sees each one in the other, without veiling or defect.
—Nuruddin Abdorahman Jami

WHO AM I?

This is the fundamental question of existence. Both science and spirituality attempt to answer this question; the whole of human history is a journey, an exploration, with the fundamental aim of knowing the source and true nature of the cosmos and ourselves.

The common thread that unites the two disciplines, objective science and subjective spirituality is consciousness. In consciousness, both the outer cosmos as explored by modern empirical science and the inner dimension of the human psyche as explored by spirituality, are simply dimensions or views arising in and from consciousness, dimensions and views that I refer to in this book as Lights of Consciousness.

All of the dimensions and views explored in this book can be seen as facets of unity, multiple faces of a single being rooted in consciousness. So what do I mean by consciousness? It is my very sense of existence, or awareness of simply being; it is that which is constant in me; despite the events and changes that occur in my life, the feeling of 'I' or 'amness' is constant. It is the feeling of consciousness itself: I AM simply consciousness.

In this book I will explore the foundations of science and spirituality and aim to present a unified view integrating the objective outer view and the subjective inner view as a science of Oneness free from conflict. I will show that all conflict is due either to dismissing one or the other as the only way of knowing, or to confusing one with the other, because each domain has its own characteristics, patterns, and methods rooted in the common space or field of consciousness.

Both science and spirituality are forms of the search for truth. One is the search for the truth of the physical world (outer/object), whereas the other is the search for the truth in the nature of consciousness (inner/subject). As such, fundamentally, there is no conflict between them, but there is the age-old problem of the 'one' and the 'many', being and form, absolute and relative, essence and appearance, mind and matter.

Originally, the search for wisdom went hand in hand with the attempt to perfect the soul. Philosophy, as a scientific discipline, has always been a way of life as well as a spiritual discipline.

Eventually, however, concern for the inner realm was relegated to theologians and moralists. Ethics was turned into an afterthought to 'real' knowledge, and fact was disjoined from value. The pre-modern traditions had sought knowledge in order to cultivate and perfect the self, but the modern scientific enterprise abandoned the self to its own subjective realm and sought to manipulate and exploit the other objective, realism.

For the same reason, historically, there has been little meeting between the two. The current scientific paradigm does not include consciousness or mind as a fundamental reality, but seeks to explain everything in physical terms. Western science, which is now by far the most dominant mode of knowledge throughout the world, has looked out to the edges of the universe, back in time to the beginning of creation, and down into the subatomic structure of matter; and it finds no place, nor need, for God. But this is because it has failed to include the inner realm of consciousness in its scope. This is now changing, and I hope to show you how science is at the dawn of exploring consciousness as fully as it has explored space, time and matter, thus creating a new world-view, one that includes spirituality.

Spirituality, on the other hand, is often perceived as unscientific in its approach to self-liberation. The perception, which is false, is that people believe things simply because someone has said it or written it down. From the scientific empirical perspective this is hardly a way to arrive at truth. It is seen as mythology rooted in dogma. The Buddha warned against this about 2,500 years ago when he said, 'Do not believe anything because I have told you it is so. Only believe it when you have tested it for yourself.' In a similar time frame the Prophet Abraham in the Middle East was the exemplar of the path of self-verification. He alone challenged the conventions of his age to emerge as the father of the great monotheistic religions.

> *Thus did We show Abraham the kingdom of the heavens and the earth that he might be of those possessing certainty.*
> *When the night grew dark upon him he beheld a star. He said: This is my Lord. But when it set, he said: I love not things that set.*
> *And when he saw the moon uprising, he exclaimed: This is my Lord. But when it set, he said: Unless my Lord guide me, I surely shall become one of the folk who are astray.*
> *And when he saw the sun uprising, he cried: This is my Lord! This is greater! And when it set he exclaimed: 'O my people! Lo! I am free from all that ye associate.*
> *I have turned my face to Him who originated the heavens and the earth, a man of pure faith; I am not of the idolaters.'*
> *His people argued with him. He said: Dispute ye with me concerning Allah when He hath guided me? I fear not at all*

> *that which ye set up beside Him unless my Lord willeth aught. My Lord includeth all things in His knowledge. Will ye not then remember?*
>
> —Qur'an 6.75-80

Spiritual science acknowledges explicitly that the meanings of things in the world cannot be found without simultaneously finding the meaning of the 'self' that knows. Certainly, one studies the world to achieve an understanding of phenomena, but understanding is an attribute of the soul, of the knowing subject. Masters of this approach recognised that meaning hides behind the 'signs' of God, that all phenomena point to noumena (noumena is in contrast to phenomena. So it's the subject in contrast to the object. It is consciousness itself without objects. The ground of experience. Or the experiencer of experience), and that those noumena can only be accessed at the root of the knowing self.

In this respect spiritual growth can be, and should be, very scientific. We can form a hypothesis that certain meditation practices enhance awareness, set up a personal experiment in meditation practice, and see what the results are. A scientific approach to spirituality is important not only in order to make sure that we do not deceive ourselves, but also to ensure that our spiritual progress is verifiable, both subjectively and objectively.

The aim of this book is to show that the scientific and spiritual quests are one and the same. The search for truth, the truth of our existence is one in which consciousness is its essential reality that drives and unifies all, at every level of existence, seen and unseen. Views from the foundations of science are presented. I will highlight the key discoveries that led to paradigm shifts in our evolution of consciousness, and show these shifts have brought us closer to the nature of reality that must exist at every level from the simple to the complex, and the inanimate to the sentient, as the sages and prophets have discovered throughout times immemorial: that of Pure Consciousness, which is the one Truth we cannot deny. It is the absolute certainty of our existence. It is eternal in that it is always there, whatever the contents

Introduction

of our experience. It is the essence of everything we know. It is the creator of our world. This is the light of God that we intuitively knew existed, but never quite found.

In the beginning, a person is conscious of one thing or another, then he is conscious that he is conscious of this thing or the other, then he is generally conscious of his consciousness, which is a prelude to pure consciousness. No one can describe pure consciousness for it is beyond ordinary experience.
—*Shaykh Fadhlalla Haeri*

The consciousness that we 'know' of is the appearance of the world. Pure Consciousness is pre-everything. *Pure*, means free from conditioning; free from cultural and religious divisions; free from the accumulation of past experiences which is memory; free from the reaction of memory which is thought; free from the movement of thought, which is time; and free from the projections of the past through the present toward the future, which is mental fragmentation and resistance of what is. When I see something for the first time, before the accumulation of memory, there is only the bewilderment and joy of the present. That is a moment of choiceless Pure Consciousness prior to the patterning of memory and the creation of thought. In the most basic terms, true freedom is freedom from the self.

The basic characteristic of Islamic intellectuality was its unitary vision. The various sciences were not understood as separate and independent realms of inquiry, but as complementary domains. The more one investigated the external world—the domain of cosmology—the more one gained insight into the internal world, the domain of spiritual psychology. The interrelationship among the fields of intellectual inquiry is especially obvious in these two realms.
—*William Chittick*

Science, or its way of investigating the universe, is an indirect affair. The true nature of the universe is forever unseen to us. We relate to existence through scientific models formulated as representations of natural phenomena that we create. A scientific 'model' is not a physical representation of a real thing; it is a mental, metaphysical image, a mathematical representation of what we 'think' it is.

A model of an atom, for example, can be a flexible sphere relating to other atoms by bouncing off each other according to a set of rules termed 'physical laws'. This basic scientific model is a mental image incorporating the essential laws of motion discovered by Isaac Newton more than 300 years ago that mark the beginning of the modern scientific age. The word *theory* derives from the Greek *theoria*, which has the same root as *theatre*, meaning 'to view' or 'to make a spectacle'. Thus, a theory is primarily a form of insight, a way of looking at the world, and not a form of knowledge of how the world is. The interpretations of nature are called theories. They are models, images of the material world made to render it comprehensible and as simple as possible.

As the Greek root of the word indicates, a hypothesis is a supposition, that is an idea that is 'put under' our reasoning, as a provisional base, which is to be tested experimentally for its truth or falsity. As is now well known, there can be no conclusive experimental proof of the truth or falsity of a general hypothesis that aims to cover the whole of reality. Rather, one finds that older theories become more and more unclear when one tries to use them to obtain insight into new domains. This is, then, generally the main clue toward new theories that constitute further new forms of insight.

With a model, it is possible to predict the various characteristics and relationships, internal and external. For example, take a system such as an atom, with its environment and defined attributes such as temperature, pressure, and force. If we conduct physical experiments and the results that we obtain match the prediction of the model, then we can say that we have a 'good' model. Of course, any experiment in itself is a 'model' of what we imagine a real system could be.

Introduction

Scientific theory cannot be so much proved as be made credible. Repeated experiments made on the basis of a theory's predictions will certainly increase its credibility but they can never prove its correctness in any absolute sense.
—Karl Popper

In the beginning, as in the case of Newton, experiments are done first to collect observations and measurements. Then the model is constructed to match the results of the experiments. So the accuracy of the model depends on the premises or the questions that the experimental model is seeking to answer, as well as on the accuracy of the observations. The next step is to use the model devised from a set of experiments to make predictions about what will happen to the same system when different experiments, based on different premises, are carried out.

If the model continues to make the 'right' predictions under new circumstances, this shows that it is a good model of what we think reality is. If it fails to make the right predictions, then either the model is wrong or modifications are required. The model may only be useful under restricted conditions, as in the case of the Newtonian model of the physical world, which applied accurately to the world.

Ultimately, all scientific models are limited. None of them are 'the truth'. We have different models for reality, based on the limits of observation and our intellectual ability. Therefore, scientific models can only be representations of reality and not reality itself, and no matter how well they work or how accurate their predictions under the appropriate circumstances, they should always be regarded as approximations and aids to the imagination, rather than ultimate truth.

The sciences are now masked; the masks lifted, they appear in all their beauty. To someone who can see the entire chain of the sciences, it would seem no harder to discern them than to do so with the sequence of all the numbers. Strict limits are prescribed for all spirits, and these limits may not be trespassed.

If some, by a flaw of spirit, are unable to follow the principles of invention, they may at least appreciate the real value of the sciences, and this should suffice to bring them true judgment on the evaluation of all things.
—Descartes

Each piece, or part, of the whole of nature is always merely an approximation to the complete truth, or the complete truth so far as we know it. In fact, everything we know is only some kind of approximation, because we know that we do not know all the laws as yet. Therefore, things must be learned only to be unlearned again or, more likely, to be corrected.
—Richard Feynman

Another way to look at it is that our scientific models are metaphors by which we relate to the world and ourselves. Mistaking the metaphor for true reality has been the bane of both scientific and religious thinking throughout human history.

The fact is that the real value of models lies in the flaws in each model, this is, where and how the model breaks down, rather than its correctness or accuracy. These flaws in each of the models that we create highlight our need for further understanding, which thus evolves and improves, allowing/assisting us to progress further in our understanding. For example, Albert Einstein's theory or model of gravity explains everything that Newton's model explains, but also explains subtle details of planetary orbits and the behaviour of light that Newton's model could not.

Science does not and cannot address the issue of understanding the true nature of the universe, because the true nature of the universe cannot be understood without reference to the transcendent, intelligent, unseen principles that govern the universe. Nor can science address the issue of how we are to find the wisdom to employ correctly the power that we gain over creation.
—William Chittick

Introduction

The same goes for spiritual science. The models the early sages and prophets used were metaphors for reality and the human condition. These metaphors were communicated in the language or representation of the time, through stories and scriptures that were also often the results of experiments within their own consciousness and that they undertook by way of meditative or contemplative practices.

The conflict between science and spirituality is often a result of mistaking the metaphors for reality itself. Modern science perceives the claims of religions as being factual descriptions of the world and ourselves, and thus spirituality is considered the domain of mythology. In truth there is no conflict or paradox. The limitations lie in our models and our imagination because we are trying to know a Reality beyond our senses, a Reality in which we are immersed and therefore can never have a totally objective view of, while we are looking at it through limited lenses that can only offer filtered and distorted views. In addition to that, we all suffer not only from our biological limitations, but also our mental limitations conditioned by culture, beliefs and vain desires. We normally prefer the familiar and reject the unfamiliar. Meanwhile, progress is always moving in the direction of exploring the unfamiliar, the unseen reality beyond our immediate comfort zone.

A complete science is a holistic enterprise that yields a unified vision. This unified vision demands the unity of the human subject with the cosmic object, that is, the conformity of the full human soul with the cosmos in all its grandeur. Self and cosmos are seen as complementary manifestations of the One, Single Principle. When God created Adam in His own image, He also created the universe in His own image. Perfect understanding means the ability to see all things in their proper places, as Divine images and in their relationship with the Source.

The conflict that exists is not between science and spirituality, which are both experiential, but between dogmatic science and religion. All knowledge claims that are settled on the basis of direct appeal to experience are identical in all genuine domains of science, physical, psychological, or spiritual. However, each domain has different characteristics, and thus the actual application of the scientific method in each domain takes on the form appropriate to that domain.

Scientists refer to those highly successful descriptions of the world as 'standard' models. Standard models are the models that describe the world from the subatomic scale, which is the domain of quantum physics, to the large-scale description of the cosmos, which is the domain of general relativity. Of course, a physical description will always be limited because it can never account for the origins of life or the nature of consciousness, and that is where a unified science of consciousness is needed.

A science of consciousness fundamentally asserts that we are, ourselves as individuals a model, an 'imaginal' representation. Philosopher Thomas Metzinger refers to this as a 'Phenomenal Self Model', a construct from and in consciousness that has been the view of spirituality all along. What we truly are and what we 'think' we are, are fundamentally different. A model is not truth. Our self-model is limited, transient, dynamic, conditioned, subject to the laws of cause and effect. Our self-model is a product of time and space, biology and culture, a complex hierarchy of values conditioned by our past histories and future expectations. As mathematician and philosopher David Deutsch says, we are always at the 'beginning of infinity' in regard to what we know, as we are an imagined entity existing within an ineffable universe.

The essence of spirituality is the search to know our true selves, to discover the real nature of consciousness. This quest has been the foundation of all the great spiritual teachings, and the goal of all the great mystics.

> *Knowers desire the Real, the First, only for His sake, not for the sake of something else.*
> —Ibn Sina (Avicenna)

Throughout the history of humanity, it has been said that the self that we know, the individual ego, is a very limited form of identity. Ignorant of our true selves, we derive a false sense of identity from what we have, or what we do, our experiences, our

Introduction

possessions, our role in the world, how others see us, and so forth. Because the world upon which our sense of self is based is continually changing, this derived sense of identity is always under threat, and our attempts to maintain it are responsible for much of our 'self-centred' behaviour.

Behind this identity is a deeper identity, what is often called the 'true self'. This can be thought of as the 'essence of consciousness'. Although our thoughts, feelings, and personality may vary considerably, the essence of consciousness remains the same. I am a different person to the one I was some years ago, but I still feel the same sense of 'I'. This sense of 'I-ness' is the same for everyone, and in that respect, it is something universal that we all share. When we discover this deeper sense of self, we are freed from many of the fears that unnecessarily plague us. We discover a greater inner peace, an inner security that does not depend upon events or circumstances in the world around us. As a result, we become less self-centred, less needy of the approval or recognition of others, less needy of collecting possessions and social status, and we become happier, healthier and more loving people. In many spiritual teachings this is called 'self-liberation'.

Most spiritual teachings also maintain that when one comes to know the true nature of consciousness, one also comes to know God. If God is the essence of the whole of creation, then the light of God is the essence of every creature and every person. This is why the search to discover the nature of one's own innermost essence is the search for God.

In summary, spiritual knowledge is that constant longing in the heart of man to have something of his origin, to experience something of his original state, the state of peace and joy that has been disturbed, and yet is sought after throughout his whole life, and never can cease to be sought after until the real source has, at length, been realised.

What was it in the wilderness that gave us peace and joy? What was it that came to us in the desert? Was it the solitude? In both cases it was nothing else but the depth of our own being, which is silent, much like the depths of the great sea, silent and still. It is the surface of the sea that makes waves and roaring breakers, much like the surface of our lives, whereas the depth of both the sea and our being are silent.

And this all-pervading, unbroken, inseparable, unlimited, ever-present, omnipotent silence unites with the silence of our being like the meeting of flames. Something from the depths of our being emerges to receive something from that all-pervading silence. Our eyes cannot see, our ears cannot hear, and our mind cannot perceive because it is beyond mind, thought, and comprehension. It is the meeting of the self and the Spirit.

In this book, I will present the nature of reality as a series of models or views that are more like meditations on the self, rooted in the science of consciousness, because any description of reality can only be communicated in a limited fashion through words. These views represent our current 'imaginal' knowledge about who we are and our place in the universe, or, more correctly, the universe's place within us.

> *Stop this day and night with me and you shall possess the origin of all poems,*
> *You shall possess the good of the earth and sun (there are millions of suns left,)*
> *You shall no longer take things at second or third hand, nor look through the eyes of the dead, nor feed on the spectres in books,*
> *You shall not look through my eyes either, nor take things from me,*
> *You shall listen to all sides and filter them from yourself.*
> —*Walt Whitman*

> *Out beyond ideas of wrong-doing and right-doing*
> *there is a field. I will meet you there.*
> *When the soul lies down in that grass,*
> *the world is too full to talk about.*
> *Ideas, language, even the phrase, each other,*
> *doesn't make any sense.*
> —*Rumi*

1 - The Fabric of Reality

To Allah belong the East and the West; whithersoever you turn, there is the Face of Allah; Allah is All-embracing, All-knowing.
—Qur'an 2.115

Existence and creation follows patterns that bring about universal interconnectedness and wholeness. The human being is a microcosm that has the potential to realize the amazing truth of one essence that energizes countless 'otherness'.
—Shaykh Fadhlalla Haeri

I marveled at an Ocean without shore, and at a Shore that did not have an ocean;
And at a Morning Light without darkness, and at a Night that was without daybreak;
And then a Sphere with no locality known to either fool or learned scholar;
And at an azure Dome raised over the earth, circulating 'round its center Compulsion;
And at a rich Earth without o'er-arching vault and no specific location, the Secret concealed.
—Ibn 'Arabi

A human being is a part of a whole, called by us 'universe', a part limited in time and space. He experiences himself, his thoughts and feelings as something separated from the rest... a kind of optical delusion of his consciousness. This delusion is a kind of prison for us, restricting us to our personal desires

> *and to affection for a few persons nearest to us. Our task must be to free ourselves from this prison by widening our circle of compassion to embrace all living creatures and the whole of nature in its beauty.*
>
> —*Albert Einstein*

Foundation

Everything we know is part of the model of reality arising as patterns or images in consciousness. This is true not only of the objects we experience in the world around us, but also the inner world of thoughts, feelings and ideas, which are likewise manifestations within consciousness, and so are the theories or models we construct about the nature of the world around us. Everything we know is structured in consciousness.

Consciousness is the fabric of reality. It is the medium from which every aspect of our experience manifests. Color, sound, taste, smell, touch, space, time, matter, every quality we ever experience in the world is a form or quality within consciousness. Our entire image of reality is generated in and from consciousness.

Consciousness is the background, or simply the ground, in the context of all experience. Whatever experience you have, whether it is a high mystical rapture, an abysmal depression, an explosive ecstasy, the sight of a bright star in a dark night's sky, the sound of thunder, the taste of honey, or the scent of roses, it all unfolds in an already dimensionless field of perfect emptiness or stillness that is the open shining matrix that lurks behind and permeates all of experience. It is consciousness.

> *No thought, no action, no movement, total stillness: only thus can one manifest the true nature and law of things from within and unconsciously, and at last become one with heaven and earth.*
>
> —*Lao Tzu*

Consciousness itself is not an altered state, or a higher station. It is not the knowing subject or an exclusive experience of any

1 - The Fabric of Reality

known object. Consciousness itself is the non-binding witness behind all arising dualities and multiplicities, and yet inherently not separate from them. It is self-existing, self-radiant, undifferentiated conscious light.

Similar claims have sometimes been made by spiritual teachings. The Western scientific mind, on the other hand, has usually dismissed such suggestions, because they do not fit in the classical scientific paradigm. However, such suggestions are only nonsensical if we confuse the two realities: the 'model reality' and true reality. We must realise that these ancient prophets and philosophers were speaking of the underlying ineffable Truth that defies all dualistic descriptions. If we consider the reality we experience, then we have to accept that in the final analysis, Consciousness is the essence of everything, everything in the known universe.

> *There was something formless and perfect before the universe was born. It is serene. Empty. Solitary. Unchanging. Infinite. Eternally present. It is the mother of the universe. For lack of a better name, I call it the Tao. It flows through all things, inside and outside, and returns to the origin of all things. The Tao is great. The universe is great. Earth is great. Man is great. These are the four great powers. Man follows the earth. Earth follows the universe. The universe follows the Tao. The Tao follows only itself.*
> —Lao Tzu

The visible material world is a shadow of the invisible spiritual world. We can say that the visible is the invisible with an energetic vibration that is perceptible by our senses, and the invisible is the visible vibrating with infinite frequencies beyond the senses. Therefore we can see that there is only Oneness behind all levels of vibrations manifesting at various layers of the seen and unseen realms. All energetic vibrations are vibrations in consciousness, which is the Oneness referred to.

And she is naught but the presence of Truth, alone, who man-

ifest Herself through forms whose every light varies.
She has manifested the unique beauty of the form design in the depth of Her being. Look at the attributes of the Beloved manifested in you.
—Shaykh Muhammad ibn al-Habib

A Universal Science

The word *science* stems from the Latin word *'scire'* meaning 'to know'. In its most general sense, science may be defined as a path to gaining reliable knowledge through careful observation and testing.

Both science and spirituality are empirical sciences. Each uses a technology that specialises in a different aspect or dimension of reality. Modern science uses the technology of sense perception as well as inductive and deductive reasoning with the aim of probing the layers of matter/energy and space/time. Spiritual science, on the other hand, uses the technology of introspection and intuitions energised by 'Divine' attributes of will, knowledge and love to probe the complex layers of the self, with the aim of revealing the underlying meaning behind the forms manifesting as thoughts, feelings and dreams. Both modern and spiritual sciences meet at the common space that is the fabric of consciousness, which, in Sufi terminology, is the *Barzakh* or inter-space. The Divine simply means the self-existing, self-radiant, conscious light of Oneness appearing as the infinite colours of attributes and actions manifesting as the world, including ourselves.

In essence they are both paths of knowledge with the ultimate goal being the realisation that the essential reality of the cosmos and the human condition is as one inseparable being existing in time and space and at the same time beyond time and space as non-dual, self-abiding consciousness. Pythagoreans, in fact, introduced the term *kosmos*, which means the patterned nature or process of all domains of existence, from matter to mind to God, and not merely the physical universe.

We can say that the purpose of spiritual practices relates to human will. This will begins as a basic need for survival based

1 - The Fabric of Reality

upon dualistic attraction and repulsion. Progressively, then, through spiritual practices, this will evolves toward its highest manifestation—to be free from the constraints of time and space, guided by the common thread of the light of consciousness immanent within all seen and unseen events in the spatio-temporal, as well as the higher realms of the multiverse.

> *Any healthy mind knows that the universe is held together by a single reality—the very word 'universe' points to this intuition (even discussion of a 'multiverse' is rooted in the unifying vision of human intelligence). The modern scientific enterprise illustrates the omnipresent intuition of tawhīd, because it is built on the assumption that knowable laws govern the universe. Any talk of laws and knowability presupposes the notion of interconnection, interrelatedness, and ultimate wholeness.*
> —William Chittick

Ultimately, spiritual maturity leads to the realisation that each domain has its appropriate technology, and thus confusing those domains leads to disastrous consequences, as evident in our history. Therefore, wisdom is the submission of our temporal human will, which in reality is always constricted, yet simultaneously inseparable from the eternal Divine will that is truly free and self-existent.

So what and where is the seat of consciousness? Where is the self, our sense of 'I-ness', located? Is it in the brain? Despite much thought and discussion, no one has yet come up with clear answers to such questions.

As with some of the other problematic issues we have looked at, this one too stems from confusing the two realities. The question that is actually being asked is 'Where is consciousness located in our image of reality?'

There are two views. The spiritual view is that consciousness is not located anywhere within the world, but rather the whole world, our entire image of reality, including our bodies and brains, is itself a manifestation within consciousness. Consciousness is the container of our world; it is not contained within it. However, we do clearly experience ourselves to be located somewhere within that image. We have created this image of reality and have quite naturally put ourselves at the centre of this image. The whole world that we have constructed is constructed around a central point: the centre of our perception.

The central point of most of our sensory experience is somewhere in the middle of the head. We see ourselves to be somewhere behind the eyes, and hear ourselves to be somewhere between the ears. This is where we quite naturally place ourselves within our image of reality. Because the brain is also located in the middle of the head, it is easy to assume that consciousness is somehow located in the brain. But this need not necessarily be so at all, as evident from the discoveries in the science of neurophysiology, which explores the correlation of brain states and consciousness, such as the phenomena of out-of-body experiences, phantom limbs, mirror neurons and so forth.

Hence, consciousness is not located anywhere within the world, but rather Consciousness is that within which the world is located. It is we who create a sense of location for ourselves within our image of the world by placing ourselves at the centre of our perceived world.

The most difficult problem, as David Chalmers, professor of philosophy, has said, is the nature of consciousness itself. Why should the complex processing of information in the brain lead to an inner experience? Why doesn't it all go on in the dark, without any subjective aspect? Why do we have any inner life at all?

It is this paradox, namely, the absolutely undeniable existence of human consciousness set against the complete absence of any satisfactory scientific account for it, that suggests that the notion of a source of consciousness in the brain is mistaken.

If consciousness is not some emergent property of matter and energy, as Western science supposes, but is instead a primary quality of the cosmos more fundamental than space, time, and matter, then we arrive at a very different picture of reality. As far as our understanding of the material world goes, nothing much changes. But when it comes to our understanding of the mind, we are led to a very different worldview, a paradigm shift in the scientific view of the universe and the human condition.

The second view on the nature of consciousness. The mainstream view of the electrochemical source of the mind, is based on the assumption that consciousness emerges from, or is dependent upon, the physical world of space, time and matter.

In one way or another, mainstream science is trying to accommodate the anomaly of consciousness within a worldview that is intrinsically materialist. As happened with the medieval astronomers, who kept adding more and more epicycles to explain the anomalous motions of the planets, the underlying assumptions are seldom, if ever, questioned.

Furthermore, due to the fact that the word *consciousness* can be used in so many different ways, confusion often arises around statements about its nature. In this book, my references to consciousness are not in reference to a particular state of consciousness, or particular way of thinking, but to the 'faculty of consciousness' itself, the capacity for inner experience, whatever the nature or degree of the experience.

> *Consciousness is an essential attribute of the Real Being, which is to say that Being and Consciousness are exactly the same in the Ultimate Reality. It is this Being-cum-Consciousness that brings forth the phenomenal universe—that is, creates the world—by means of various attributes that are self-evident in our experience of ourselves and the universe, such as life, power, and love.*
>
> —William Chittick

A useful analogy described by Peter Russell, a scientist and philosopher, is that of an image from a video projector. The projector shines light onto a screen. Modifying the light enables us to produce any one of an infinity of images. These images are like the perceptions, sensations, dreams, memories, thoughts and feelings that we experience—what I call the 'contents of consciousness.' The light itself, without which no images would be possible, corresponds to the faculty of consciousness. We know all the images on the screen are composed of this light, but we are not usually aware of the light itself. Our attention is caught up in the images that appear and the stories they tell. In much the same way, we know we are conscious, but we are usually aware only of the many different experiences, thoughts, and feelings that appear in the mind. We are seldom aware of consciousness itself. Yet without this faculty there would be no experience of any kind.

Light is often the preferred model of spiritual traditions to describe consciousness. It transcends the world of space and time, it is self-evident, and everything else is simply infinite shadows pointing back as signs and metaphors to that original light.

All authentic traditions of spirituality have been associated with an understanding of the structures underlying human experience. This understanding is based on detailed knowledge of the nervous system, of the various organs within the body, and so forth. It has always been associated with an analysis of the human structure, of the workings of that structure, and the methods by which the esoteric practitioner can make use of that structure in the process of realisation.

Through the entire collective human process of examining the nature of conditionally manifested existence, a single great principle is made evident: All manifestation arises from a prior and inherently indivisible unity. Everything that appears is developed from what is already there, inherently and potentially. Therefore it is false philosophy to presume that reality is reducible to the observable 'facts' of the presumed separate human structure and its functioning.

Our psycho-physical structure is irreducibly part of this universal unity. Reality is non-separate, indivisible and one beyond appearances. Thus, our psycho-physical structure is the 'vehicle' that can be used by us on the path to self-realisation, and that structure arises within the universal unity.

> *Only that which is objective can be dependent upon the law of causation, can be an effect of cause, or can experience the effect of causes. The process of cause–effect is dependent on time*

(duration) and necessarily is phenomenal; therefore every phenomenon must be dependent on temporal causation. That which is dependent on causation, being the result of causes, no volitional element can interfere with the operation of this process, and there cannot be any entity therein to exercise 'freedom of will'. On the other hand non-objectivity can never be dependent on causation, and, not being phenomenal, can never be bound, or ever suffer any experience. Moreover whatever is non-objective cannot be an entity (which is an objective concept), and so there cannot be any noumenal exercise of volition either, and there can be no 'will' to be bound or to be free. Volition (acts of 'will'), therefore, necessarily are illusory; they can only be an apparent interference in the operation of causality that inevitably is ineffectual. Thus 'purpose' and 'intention' on the part of an imaginary entity can only find fulfillment or frustration when they are in accordance with, or in opposition to, an effect of causation, and such frustration or fulfillment can only be psychological phenomena.
—Wei Wu Wei

Manifest Hierarchy

The single, supreme Principle manifests itself through multiplicity, but this is an ordered and hierarchical multiplicity, one that begins with twoness and gradually differentiates itself into various cosmic levels. Twoness is an especially important notion in cosmological thinking, because it allows us to conceive of a world along with the supreme One. The duality that appears when we conceptualize the world next to God colors all the relationships between the One and the many and has repercussions throughout the cosmos.
—William Chittick

Philosophers like Alfred North Whitehead and Ken Wilber argued that consciousness goes all the way down. It is an intrinsic property of creation. From this perspective, what has emerged as life has evolved is not the faculty of consciousness, but the various qualities evolved, and dimensions of conscious experience—the contents of consciousness. As living beings evolved, the patterns that were painted in consciousness became increasingly richer. To process and use this information, nervous systems evolved, and as the nervous systems grew more complex, new qualities emerged, such as free will, cognition, intention and attention. With the appearance of human beings, consciousness gained an entirely new dimension: thinking.

This way, all creation can be said to have the faculty of consciousness as the underlying principle, differing only in the capacity and degree of manifestation of attributes already embedded in consciousness. Everything manifests as a spectrum of consciousness.

It is probable that any organism that is sensitive in some way to its environment has a degree of interior experience. If a bacterium is sensitive to physical vibration, light intensity or heat, who are we to say it does not have a corresponding degree of consciousness? The picture that is painted might be the equivalent of an extremely faint smudge of colour, virtually nothing, compared to the richness and detail of human experience, but not completely non-existent. How far down do we go? Would the same apply to viruses and DNA? Even to crystals and atoms?

That is certainly the view of Ken Wilber, who developed a model of consciousness based on the perennial philosophy that is the basis of all wisdom traditions. The main premise is that the whole of existence can be described as a great chain of being where manifest existence represents one dimension of a multi-dimensional universe that has an exterior observable objective dimension as well as an interior subjective dimension.

The objective dimension has been the domain of the natural sciences, and the subjective, the domain of the spiritual and religious sciences. Each can be seen as the expression of one truth, one being, and one self. One truth and multiple realities are experienced exteriorly and interiorly through the agency of consciousness. Confusing these dimensions or reducing them to one or the other results in fragmented and divided worldviews preventing a vision of a unified and holistic Cosmos.

1 - The Fabric of Reality

Cosmos here refers to the totality of human experience, interior and exterior, individual and collective, as revealed by the great wisdom traditions and elaborated in the integral philosophy of Ken Wilber in the present post-post-modern age of ours.

The universe is seen as composed of a hierarchy of nests or spheres within spheres of indefinite *holons*, an integral state of whole/parts. These holons express the fundamental duality and ambiguity, a form of mutually interrelated patterns and processes emerging as a hierarchy from an absolute state of infinite potentiality. These holons emerge and take form as a multitude of dualities, in distinctive phases of an evolving universe that are comprehensible by the agency of human consciousness that represents the pinnacle expression of this a multidimensional Cosmos. Each phase or reality transcends and includes the attributes and properties of the previous phase. The new properties are emergent properties that include, but are not reducible to, the previous ones. Biology transcends and includes physics, but is not reducible to the laws of physics, thereby representing a new level of being with its own distinctive qualities and contexts.

Evolution of the Cosmos is seen as self-realisation through self-transcendence. Evolution is a self-transcending process in that it has the capacity to go beyond what went before, incorporating the past and then adding novel components. The drive for self-transcendence thus appears to be built into the very fabric of the Cosmos itself: the appearance of novelty, emergence, creativity, new entities coming into being, new patterns unfolding, new holons issuing forth. This process builds unions out of fragments. The Cosmos unfolds in quantum leaps of creative emergence. The creative Spirit is the ultimate ground that gives rise to form. Out of sheer emptiness or stillness, manifestation arises. Manifestation occurs in a natural hierarchy that is simply an order of increasing wholeness, such as is seen in the natural hierarchal order of particles to atoms to cells to organisms.

The whole of one level becomes a part of the whole of the next. Each emergent holon transcends but includes its predecessors. *Transcends* means that a holon has emergent or novel creative properties that are not merely the sum of its parts. New levels of organisation come into being that cannot be reduced to the previous dimension.

Spirit, or pure consciousness, transcends all, so it includes all. It is beyond this world, but utterly embraces every single holon. It permeates all of manifestation, but is not merely manifestation. It is ever present at every level or dimension. It is both the highest level and the tablet on which the entire hierarchy is written. It is both the goal and the ground of the entire sequence. Evolution has a broad tendency to move in the direction of increasing complexity, increasing differentiation/integration, increasing organisation and patterning, and increasing relative autonomy.

The greater the depth of the holon, the greater its consciousness. There is a spectrum of consciousness, and evolution unfolds that spectrum. Consciousness unfolds, thereby realising itself into manifest existence. Evolution is both transcendence and immanence. It is immanent in the process itself, woven into the very fabric of the Cosmos; but it transcends its own productions everywhere, and brings forth anew in every moment. Depth increases from subconscious to self-conscious to super-conscious, on the way to its own recognition, utterly one with the radiant All.

The Cosmos can also be seen as a model of consciousness unfolding on various levels or waves from physical to biological to cognitive to spiritual, passing through various developmental psychological lines or streams representing the interior dimension of our objective universe. In effect, everything we know about the universe has much to do with levels of consciousness as with the objective manifest universe observed and studied by the natural sciences. The manifest universe is not Spirit or pure consciousness but a symbol or a manifestation of Spirit. It is also not strictly matter, but the organisation of energy expressed in a multitude of forces emerging in phases or realities represented mainly by quantum reality and classical reality.

We know this through the agency of our consciousness, which makes use of outer sensory tools in effect, conditions and obscures, the true nature of the Cosmos as consciousness. A transcendental level of consciousness is required to disclose itself, revealing the one truth behind the multiple realities. Essentially, truth transcends and includes multiple realities. It is the origin and end of all endeavours, uniting and integrating the seemingly fragmented and contradictory dimensions and domains of existence.

The hierarchy of the Cosmos is a model of a ranking of orders of events according to their holistic capacity. What is whole at one stage becomes a part of a larger whole at the next stage. Originally, it was a mystical notion of celestial orders, representing higher (or deeper) knowledge and virtue, and illuminations that were accessible in contemplative awareness. The whole or context can determine the meaning and function of a part. The whole is more than the sum of its parts, and the whole can influence and determine the function of its parts. Hierarchy is a fundamental structural principle of the Cosmos. It unfolds in asymmetrical order of increasing wholeness, it is not reversible. Parts within each level relate hierarchically. Between hierarchical levels, downward causation (higher influences, lower, mind influences, body, e.g.) and upward causation are also possible.

Hierarchies unfold to actualise the latent potentials in entities forming greater wholes. Pathology exists when a holon assumes it's a whole only or a part only. We exist in various contexts (holons), which unavoidably constitute various values and meanings that are embedded in our conditions because we ourselves are holons embodying a value hierarchy. It is impossible to live without a context, without qualitative discriminations or value hierarchies.

All forms are fundamentally forms in consciousness, lower (quarks and below) or upper limit (self and above). Consciousness displays itself qualitatively as a spectrum of shifting shades whose lower terms are lost in the night.

Outer holons	**Inner holons**
Atoms	Prehension
Cells	Irritability
Plants	Rudimentary sensation
Proto-neuronal (jellyfish)	Sensation

Neuronal (worms)   Perception
Neural cord (fish)   Perception/impulse
Brain stem (reptiles)   Impulse/emotion
Limbic system (dinosaurs) Emotion/image
Neocortex (primates)   Symbols
Complex neocortex (humans) Concepts

Similarly, in Islamic Sufi cosmology, we see a hierarchical model. The basic understanding is that the Cosmos is coherent, ordered, layered and directional. There are degrees of reality, some closer to Real Being and some further away. Closeness to the Real is judged in terms of the degree of participation in its attributes, that is, by the intensity of a level's unity, life, consciousness, power, will, compassion, wisdom, love, and so on. Distance from the Real is judged by the weakness of these same attributes. Ultimately, the traces of Being–Consciousness become so attenuated that the process can go no further, so it turns back upon itself. The universe can be seen as bidirectional, eternally coming forth from the One and eternally receding back into the One. It is at once centrifugal and centripetal. The Real is Absolute, Infinite, and Unchanging, and everything else is moving, altering, and transmuting. All movement is either toward the Real or away from it. The direction of movement is judged in terms of the increasing or decreasing intensity of the signs and traces of the Real that appear in things.

Despite these two movements, centrifugal and centripetal, descending and ascending, consciousness itself never leaves its own invisible and transcendent reality. In its deepest nature, the human self is indistinguishable from its ground in consciousness, so it remains indefinable and non-specific. Every specific thing and every specific viewpoint tells the self what it is not. The self knows that it is not limited by the objects of its knowledge or by the finiteness of things, nor by the limitations of this standpoint or that science. It also knows that it has the potential to perceive and comprehend all definitions and all limitations.

Reality is understood in terms of continuums, spectrums,

1 - The Fabric of Reality

complementarities, equilibriums, balances, and unities. Spirit or soul and body, heaven and earth, past and future, local and non-local, all are understood as relative and complementary terms. There is also an intermediate between any duality, which plays the role of an 'isthmus' or *barzakh*, something that is neither the one nor the other but allows for interrelationship.

The first reality that the Supreme Reality brings into existence, the Intellect or Spirit, is as similar to that Reality as any contingent thing can be. It is aware with a contingent awareness of all that may possibly be. The Real gives rise to multiplicity by means of this first, contingent reality. But the universe appears gradually and, as it moves further from its origin, becomes ever more diminished, just as the intensity of light decreases in keeping with its distance from its source. This diminution of reality occurs in a series of stages that are enumerated in a variety of ways.

Consciousness is not an emergent quality, because the inner does not emerge from the outer. They both emerge together from the first boundary, the creation of the universe, from the very first differentiation of the Cosmos into an inner and an outer. Consciousness has an inner depth at every stage, and is not something that emerges at some stage down the line. Forms of consciousness emerge as forms of energy/matter, but consciousness itself is simply alongside all along, as the principal reality of every form. The inner and outer are co-emergent from the start. Consciousness is the openness, the emptiness, of the holons that allows qualities to emerge.

We are inescapably situated in relation to the three domains:

1. The inner subjective world, the zone of truthfulness, sincerity, beauty and art;
2. The outer objective world, the zone of empirical science; and
3. The intersubjective world of society and culture, the zone of rightness, justice, ethic and morality.

Each of these domains has its own claim to validity and its own standards, and none of them can be reduced to the other.

Fragmented science is the attempt to reduce the Cosmos to one of the domains as the only truth, where truth no longer means attunement with the Cosmos, but merely how to map the Cosmos functionally, independently without purpose. Similarly, personal integrity, intentions, and meaning are reduced to healthy brain functioning and behavioural modifications. Cultural meaning is reduced to social integration. Likewise, cultural values are meaningful only to the extent that they promote social cohesion.

The faculty of consciousness is the one thing we all share, but what goes on in our consciousness, that is, the content of our consciousness, varies widely. This is our personal reality, the reality we each know and experience. Most of the time, however, we forget that this is just our personal reality and think we are experiencing physical reality directly. I see the ground beneath my feet, I can pick up a rock and throw it through the air, I feel the heat from a fire and can smell its burning wood. It feels as if I am in direct contact with the world 'out there'. But that is not so. The colors, textures, smells and sounds that I experience are not really 'out there'. They are all images of reality constructed in my mind. As Fred Alan Wolf says: 'There is no out there, out there'.

Because our perception of the world is so different from the actual physical reality, some people have claimed that our experience is an illusion. However, that is misleading. It may all be a creation of our own minds, but it is very, very real—the only reality we will ever know. The illusion comes when we confuse our experience of the world with the physical reality, the thing-in-itself. The Vedantic philosophers of ancient India spoke of this as *maya*. Often translated as *illusion* (a false perception of the world), the word is more accurately translated as *delusion* (a false belief about the world). I suffer a delusion when I believe that the manifestations in my mind are the external world. I deceive myself when I think that the tree I see is the tree itself.

If all that we ever know are the images that appear in our

1 - The Fabric of Reality

minds, then how can we be sure there is a physical reality behind our perceptions? Is it not just an assumption? My answer to that is: Yes, it is an assumption. Nevertheless, it seems a most plausible assumption. For a start, there are definite constraints on my experience. I cannot, for example, walk through walls. If I try to, there are predictable consequences. Nor can I, when awake, float through the air or walk upon water.

Second, my experience generally follows well-defined laws and principles: balls thrown through the air follow precisely defined paths, cups of coffee cool at similar rates, the sun rises on time. Furthermore, this predictability is not peculiar to my personal reality. You, whom I assume to exist, report similar patterns in your own experience. The simplest way, by far, of accounting for these constraints and for their consistency is to assume that there is indeed an objective reality. We may not know it directly, and its nature may be nothing like our experience of it, but it is there.

Only the disposition or viewpoint of 'no viewpoint' can allow for transcending viewpoints and arriving at the meaning behind all relative and situational meanings. The viewpoint of 'no viewpoint' is available only in the transcendent realm that gives rise to the universe in the first place. True meaning can never be grasped by dogma, doctrine, theories, theorems, or any other mental construct. It can only be found by going beyond the operations of conditioned consciousness, actualising the unitary pure consciousness, the primordial intelligence that lies beneath the mind and behind the world, and integrating the human self, back into its transcendent origin.

> 'Truth is a pathless land'. Man cannot come to it through any organization, through any creed, through any dogma, priest or ritual, not through any philosophical knowledge or psychological technique. He has to find it through the mirror of relationship, through the understanding of the contents of his own mind, through observation and not through intellectual analysis or introspective dissection.

Man has built in himself images as a fence of security—religious, political, personal. These manifest as symbols, ideas, beliefs. The burden of these images dominates man's thinking, his relationships, and his daily life. These images are the causes of our problems for they divide man from man. His perception of life is shaped by the concepts already established in his mind. The content of his consciousness is his entire existence. The individuality is the name, the form and superficial culture he acquires from tradition and environment. The uniqueness of man does not lie in the superficial but in complete freedom from the content of his consciousness, which is common to all humanity. So he is not an individual.
—J.Krishnamurti

Mankind has the potential of being conscious of pure consciousness, or even non-consciousness, without being completely knocked out by the knowledge or experience of this. In other words, you are a pure slate of consciousness before any other consciousness arose, before your upbringing changed you and agitated you, a consciousness without which you would not be alive. The world is based on change, movement and energy, which can only be measured against a pure slate. Our senses are tested and activated in order for us to explore and discover our own mini kingdom—the kingdom of our body and mind, heart and soul. This, in turn, is so that we discover Allah's kingdom. Then whatever role or action we perform we are in unison with it and content with every moment of our destiny.
—Shaykh Fadhlalla Haeri

2 - The View of Origins

Allah originates creation, then brings it back again, then unto Him you shall be returned. —Qur'an 30.11

Beginnings

To speak of origins normally means a beginning in time and a location in space where the universe or the self emerges from an 'imaginal' singular point of 'view' that 'explodes' and 'expands' in time and space. From the spiritual timeless and spaceless point of view, origins are effulgences from non-time and non-space appearing as the tapestry of existence within the void of Pure Consciousness. It important to understand the nature of appearances: how can there be appearances in timelessness? And to what do they appear?

A prophetic tradition says, 'I was a hidden treasure and loved to be known so I created'. The unfathomable, mysterious hidden depth of Pure Consciousness is absolute and infinite, 'infinite' meaning that it potentially contains all limitations as well as the possibility of negating its timeless nature, which then can virtually appear as an 'other', like a dream ripple in the depth of consciousness.

Everything in the universe is made of consciousness, and nothing is created without it. As consciousness becomes manifest as Life and existent as Pure Consciousness, it makes patterns and forms of itself and becomes an appearance: the measurable total of all things present and knowable within the fabric of Pure Consciousness. Whereas the universe contains all things that were and will be, the appearance is a unique perspective of the

Universe, created by introducing the dimension of time.

The appearance is like a snapshot of this process of manifestation, but one that is forever in the process of change. The appearance is Now. Therefore it is said that the appearance is a state of perpetual impermanence: the appearance is shaped and reshaped by these processes, whereas Pure Consciousness remains whole. The appearance never stops changing and moving, whereas Pure Consciousness is changeless and unmoved. The patterns and forms of the appearance, also called objects, are created within Pure Consciousness, they exist within Pure Consciousness and they return to the source, which they never really left. In passing through the appearance, Pure Consciousness achieves the perfect state of balance between existence and non-existence, perfect mutability and perfect changelessness.

Before anything in the universe was Pure Consciousness 'Is'. The appearance is its "Isness" in the form of a three-dimensional universe is made present by the dimension of time. Hence, the perception from a direction of measurement 'beyond' or 'within' those available to a psychic apparatus, such further direction being cognised as duration, is a phenomenon known as *form*.

The appearance can be likened to a vast ocean in which all things exist. At this level of perception, the ocean appears to be empty, because all things that exist are made of the ocean water (Life). They are not merely in the ocean, but are of the ocean: the manifest and existent energy of Pure Consciousness that takes form as the appearance. As the water moves in three dimensions, it creates patterns and forms that appear on a large scale as tides and currents, and on a smaller scale as individual waves and, smaller yet, as drops of water. These patterns and forms are the beginning of what we recognize as substantial objects that have a place and time within the universe. They are created of water, exist as water while they appear, and dissolve back into the water. They never cease to be all by the power of the manifest life in motion. The ocean is the water, and all the tides and currents and waves and drops are now. Objects rise and objects vanish; the ocean alone is real. Therefore, it can be comprehended that form is not a structure as such *within* a dimensional *framework*,

2 - The View of Origins

as may have been supposed, but is in fact an appearance *whose composition consists entirely of directions of measurement* perceived from the source.

No object can understand its place within the mystery of Pure Consciousness that brings it forth and calls it back to the source; this is like asking a single wave to direct the tides, or a drop of water to know the entire ocean. But just as the tides and currents work with gravitational forces to move the ocean waters, Pure Consciousness moves everything in the appearance from within and from without. However, Pure Consciousness moves within them and pulls from beyond them, so the patterns and forms of the appearance exist and move without knowing what they do. These objects are not aware of themselves, but one drop cannot fail to recognize another drop as water, the life which is common to both. Thus, no objects of the appearance are separate from each other. Each drop is a conscious projection of the universe, existing simultaneously as part and whole. No matter how infinitesimally small within the ocean, each drop of water, while present, never ceases also to be the entire ocean.

In not recognising themselves as separate objects with a function (relative motion through the appearance), the patterns and forms of the appearance therefore retain an undivided consciousness of their source. As the totality of their function is unknown to them, these objects simply project the presence of Pure Consciousness as they are moved through the appearance like drops of water pulled by the tides. The dimension of time creates their distinctive spatial relations (and therefore their function as well), but these objects are not conscious of time, only of the now in which they are present as the ocean.

Thus we say that the appearance, just as the life and the universe of Pure Consciousness, exists as one without a two. There is no second appearance to contrast with the one that is now. The appearance knows only this Unity. It does not know itself as the many patterns and forms because it does not exist as a pair of ones that can observe each other. This is the secret to its perfection. The objects of the appearance simply perform the function for which they were formed in the potency of the life and by the light of Pure Consciousness, and dissolve back into the non-manifest mystery. But at no point do these objects have any reality or function outside of Pure Consciousness, which is always one. Thus, the hidden mystery and the life and universe of Pure Consciousness are one with all present objects of the appearance, although the three give birth to the many.

Thus we can say that the knowable universe emerges through a process of contraction within Pure Consciousness and successive boundary creation descending from the timeless and spaceless, described in the Qur'an as the seven heavens, toward what we know as the visible universe. The origin of the universe, as we know it, represents a process of evolution in time and space that culminated in the emergence of human consciousness, which has the ability to ascend back, not through, time and space. But through journeying within uncovering the layers thereby reveals the depths of its own consciousness towards its core being: the heart, which is the seat of consciousness, and comes to know its ever-present timeless origin as Pure Consciousness beyond all limitations and boundaries.

Learning to observe is the beginning of knowledge and science. The earliest observations were passive and non-discriminatory. It all began with observing our separate existence. Then moving objects gave us the sense of outer existence. Movement caught our eyes and told secrets of the natural order of things.

Our basic consciousness began with the subtle division between the self and the outside world. A process of thinking. A process of analysis and synthesis led to distinction, which is a separation of 'out there' from the 'in here'. This is called subject–object distinction. Consciousness begins with the awareness of 'I am'. That 'in here' experience is necessary before any real observation can take place.

The first observations of the early Greeks considered two conflicting ways of understanding the human condition: either all was one or all was change. The first hypothesis is based on the 'I' experience, which is the only experience that each of us knows for sure. And everything else is an illusion. The conflicting view is that all is change, and the awareness of 'I' is the illusion. Thus

2 - The View of Origins

arose the conflict between change and being. Out of this debate arose the very spirit of science. The word physics comes from the Greek word *physis* meaning the essential essence of all things.

A Brief History of Time

In the sixteenth century, a new spirit of enquiry had appeared. It was the start of the mechanical age, or the age of reason. The science of the passive observer had ended, and the active observer was eager to explore and take things apart. The 'whole' observed by the Greeks was always more than the sum of its parts. The 'whole' envisioned during the mechanical age exactly equals the sum of its parts. Laws of conservation arose, and mass or matter and energy were understood to be conserved. The world of physics became simpler by studying the parts, and by piecing the parts together physicists found they could understand any complex motion.

Newton's laws of motion were the supreme laws of the universe based on the assumption that the observer does not disturb. He only observes what is there. And Newton's laws predicted a strange kind of symmetry where the laws would work running backward or forward in time. From any given moment in time, the future was completely determined and could be predicted. Also the past could be reconstructed. Past, present and future are continuously connected by deterministic laws. By the nineteenth century, the mechanical age of reason had become the age of certainty.

The age of reason relied heavily on the philosophy of René Descartes who returned to the old 'being versus change' argument. He recognised that he thought, and he concluded logically that he existed. His awareness that he existed was his only proof of his own existence. Descartes recognised that being and change were complementary. All was neither total being nor total change. 'I am' meant being. 'I think' meant change. Therefore being was the background for change, and change was necessary for awareness of one's existence. This was the foundation for logical thought in the age of reason. Descartes made a bold attempt to construct a complete theory of the universe using nothing but the elements of being and change. These were called matter and motion. He saw motion as relative not absolute. The problem was one of perspective.

The first prime example of the modern physicist is Galileo Galilei. He devised methods of observation, description and analysis that today we accept as the basis for all physics. His essential contribution was the replacement of the passive observer with the active observer. Isaac Newton was able to bring together the concepts of passive observation and active observation. Active observation was, for Newton, an extension of passive observation. Instruments simply detected. They did not alter the existing world that they explored.

The cross-fertilisation of mathematics with experimental methods was resulting in major insights. Scientists were looking up into the universe and peering down into the tiniest objects observable. Based upon Descartes philosophy, mind was distinct from matter. Therefore the observer was distinct from the observed.

Following Descartes, philosophy of modern cosmology, the view that came to be known as the 'Big Bang' asserts that the entire universe is an expression of the sheer void of undifferentiated singleness. A remarkable feature of the present universe is that the sum of all the energy in the universe almost adds up to zero. First, there is the potential energy of the gravitational attraction of the galaxies for each other. This is proportional to the mass of the galaxies. To push the galaxies apart, a huge negative energy is required to counteract the attractive force. If the two forces add up, then the total energy in the universe would be zero, and it would not take any energy to create the universe. Astronomers are searching for the 'missing mass' that is not so far accounted for.

Quantum physics tells us that this apparent emptiness is the source of all matter/energy. Elementary particles simply spontaneously form into existence. This paradox of empty fullness is the ground of the universe. The action of the origin is not confined to the distant past. It is a ceaseless action throughout the universe, this shining forth and dissolving back into an ever-present origin.

2 - The View of Origins

The present view of the beginning of creation, what became called the 'standard Big Bang model', states that the entire universe originated in an enormous explosion. All matter, the stars and galaxies were once concentrated into a very hot, dense primordial 'matter soup'. This matter soup expanded rapidly and it exploded. Not an explosion like those familiar on earth, starting from a definite centre and spreading out to engulf more and more of the circumambient air, but an explosion that occurred simultaneously everywhere, filling all space from the beginning, with every particle of matter rushing apart from every other particle. 'All space' in this context may mean either all of an infinite universe, or all of a finite universe that curves back on itself like the surface of a sphere.

The first energy/particle interactions were not fixed and determined. There was freedom and randomness, and there were no identifiable objects or events. This first phase reached its end when the freely symmetric interactions formed into a structure, an identifiable pattern. A new phase had begun. What had been free was now fixed into particular interactions with determined intensities. These early patterns will unfold gradually into the four known physical fields or forces—the gravitational, the electromagnetic and the two nuclear interactions—forming fields within fields, contexts within contexts, with new emergent patterns unfolding, forming greater and greater complexity and allowing numerous relationships and interactions with wider spans and greater depths.

In the primordial fireball, the latent heat released by the phase transitions generated new particles that emerged briefly and then annihilated, contingent evanescent beings appearing in a flash for a moment then disappearing back into the void of non-existence. The seeds of space and time were formed in these early ripples of its fundamental constituents flaring from the underlying fabric of non-space-time.

At about one-hundredth of a second, the earliest time about which we can speak with any confidence, the temperature of the universe was about 100 billion degrees Kelvin. This is hotter than the centre of the hottest star. So hot, in fact, that none of the components of ordinary matter, molecules, or atoms, or even the nuclei of atoms, could have held together. Instead, the matter rushing apart in this explosion consisted of various types of the so-called elementary particles, electrons, positron, photons, neutrinos and anti-neutrinos. These particles were continuously being created and destroyed as they interacted.

After the first tenth of a second, the universe cooled down to about 10 billion degrees Kelvin, and after 14 seconds to about 1 billion degrees. This was cool enough to take the electrons and positrons out of equilibrium with photons and neutrinos, and now if positrons were annihilated they would not be recreated. This was the first symmetry break that allowed matter to dominate the universe, rather than antimatter. All that remained were electrons, neutrinos, and photons, with a small contamination of protons and neutrons.

After three minutes, the universe cooled enough for the protons and neutrons to form nuclei. These were the lightest nuclei of helium and deuterium. The helium created is about 27 percent of all matter in the universe. After about a 100,000 years, the temperature dropped sufficiently for the electrons to combine with the nuclei to form atoms. Great clouds of atoms began to condense into stars and galaxies. Inside the stars, the heavier elements like carbon and iron got cooked up from hydrogen and helium by a process called nucleosynthesis. After a few billion years the universe began to look like its present state.

A star begins to form as a dense cloud of gas in the arms of a spiral galaxy. Individual hydrogen atoms fall with increasing speed and energy toward the centre of the cloud under the force of the cloud's gravity. The increase in energy heats the gas. When this process has continued for some millions of years, the temperature reaches about 20 million degrees Fahrenheit. At this temperature, the hydrogen within the star ignites and burns in a continuing series of nuclear reactions. The onset of these reactions marks the birth of a star.

When a star begins to exhaust its hydrogen supply, its life nears an end. The first sign of a star's old age is a swelling and reddening of its outer regions. Such an aging, swollen star is

2 - The View of Origins

called a *red giant*. Our Sun is a middle-aged star that is estimated will swell to a red giant in 5 billion years, vaporising Earth and any creatures that may be on its surface. When all its fuel has been exhausted, a star cannot generate sufficient pressure at its centre to balance the crushing force of gravity. The star collapses under the force of its own weight. If it is a small star, then it collapses gently and remains collapsed. Such a collapsed star, at its life's end, is called a *white dwarf*. Our Sun will probably end its life in this way.

A different fate awaits a large star. Its final collapse generates a violent explosion called a *supernova*, blowing the innards of the star out into space. The materials of the exploded star mix with the primeval hydrogen of the universe. Later in the history of the galaxy, other stars are formed out of this mixture. Our Sun was one of those stars. It contains the debris of countless other stars that exploded before it was born.

A remnant of a supernova is what is known as a *neutron star* which is one of the possible ends for a star. Neutron stars result from massive stars that have mass greater than 4 to 8 times that of our Sun. After these stars have finished burning their nuclear fuel, they undergo a supernova explosion. This explosion blows off the outer layers of a star into a beautiful supernova remnant. The central region of the star collapses under gravity with such force that protons and electrons combine to form neutrons—hence the name *neutron star*.

A rotating neutron star is called a *pulsar*, because it appears to pulse as it rotates. Pulsars are spinning neutron stars that have jets of particles moving almost at the speed of light streaming out above their magnetic poles. These jets produce very powerful beams of light. For a similar reason that 'true north' and 'magnetic north' are different on Earth, the magnetic and rotational axes of a pulsar are also misaligned. Therefore, the beams of light from the jets sweep around as the pulsar rotates, just as the spotlight in a lighthouse does. Like a ship in the ocean that sees only regular flashes of light, we see pulsars 'turn on and off' as the beam sweeps over the Earth.

When stars that are more than 20 times the size of our Sun

end their lives in a supernova explosion, their cores collapse and gravity wins out over any other force that might be able to hold the star up. Eventually, the star collapses so much that it is contained within its *event horizon*, the boundary within which light cannot escape, forming a *black hole*. At this point, the black hole is extremely tiny. A black hole with the mass of the Sun would fit in a small town, while one with the mass of the Earth would fit in the palm of your hand! The material inside the event horizon will continue to collapse indefinitely, reaching the point where our understanding of the laws of physics breaks down. No information from inside the event horizon can escape to the outside world.

Supermassive black holes, meanwhile, form differently, perhaps from the merger of many smaller black holes early in the universe's history, and such black holes grow over the years as they suck in gas from their surroundings. The formation of these objects and their relationship to the galaxy that harbours them is still an area of active research.

We can't observe black holes directly, but we do see their effect on surrounding materials such as gas and dust which let out their last gasp before being sucked into the black hole or flung away in a jet. Black holes, in fact, are extremely efficient at converting the energy of incoming materials into emitted light. The gas that falls into a black hole does not plunge in directly, for the same reason the Earth does not plunge into the Sun. Instead, it tries to move around the black hole in an orbit, forming what is known as an *accretion disk*. These energetic black holes are known as *quasars*.

Material in the accretion disk slowly spirals inward as it loses energy due to friction—the huge gravitational tides near the black hole are excellent at ripping apart this material and heating it to high temperatures. The inner disks of supermassive black holes reach thousands of degrees Kelvin (similar to the temperatures at the surface of a hot star), whereas smaller black holes can heat their disks to millions of degrees, where they emit radiation in the x-ray part of the spectrum.

Quasars, therefore, are some of the brightest objects around.

2 - The View of Origins

Quasars can be detected out near the edge of the visible universe, where they shine with the brightness of trillions of Suns. Micro-quasars in our own galaxy can easily be hundreds of thousands of times brighter than the Sun, even though they are typically only 10 times as massive.

It is thought that the centre of a black hole is a singularity. A *singularity* means a point where a property such as mass is infinite. At the centre of a black hole, according to classical theory, the density is infinite because a finite mass is compressed to zero volume. Hence, it is a singularity. Similarly, if you extrapolate the properties of the universe back in time to the instant of the Big Bang, then you will find that both the density and the temperature go to infinity and so that is also a singularity.

The age of the universe today, or, more precisely, the measurable universe, is estimated to be around 13.8 billion years old. Around 5 billion years ago in a perfectly ordinary place in the galaxy, a supernova exploded, pushing a lot of its heavy-element wreckage into a nearby cloud of hydrogen gas and interstellar dust. The mixture grew hot and compressed under its own gravity, and at its centre a new star began to form. Around it swirled a disk of the same material, which grew white-hot from the great compressive forces. That new star became our Sun, and the glowing disk gave rise to Earth and its sister planets.

As time went by, planetesimals grew by collision with other bodies, and as the mass of each planetismal grew larger, the energies involved did too. By the time they reached 100 kilometres or so in size, planetesimal collisions produced a lot of outright melting and vaporisation, and materials, such as rock and iron metal began to sort themselves out. The dense iron settled in the centre and the lighter rock separated into a mantle around the iron, in a miniature of Earth and the other inner planets today. The Earth is around 4 billion years old, and life on Earth emerged around 2.5 billion years ago. At one point early in this process a very large planetesimal struck Earth an off-centre blow and sprayed much of Earth's rocky mantle into space. The planet got most of it back after a period of time, but some of it collected into a second planetesimal circling Earth, which we call the Moon.

The Big Bang model became the standard model of creation following two important discoveries. The first discovery was that of the expansion of the universe by Edwin Hubble in 1929. He observed that the *red shift* of the light from distant galaxies is proportional to their distance from us. A galaxy that is moving away at high speed has its spectral lines of light shifted to the red in proportion to its speed. This is called a *Doppler shift*. This meant that the universe is expanding at a uniform rate.

The second discovery was the detection of microwave background radiation by Arno Penzias and Robert Wilson in 1964. They found that the distant empty universe is not absolutely cold. It has a slight temperature of three degrees Kelvin above absolute zero. This temperature is due to the radiation of photons that permeate all of space. This radiation is the heat left over from the Big Bang.

Before the first hundredth of a second, there can only be speculations as to the nature of the universe due to the enormous temperature and uncertainty. The distinction between all interactions is lost. It was a universe of perfect symmetry. Perfect symmetry means equal amounts of matter and antimatter which always form pure energy. Nothing can emerge from that unless this symmetry is somehow broken.

Invariance

Another recent point of view was proposed by mathematical cosmologist Roger Penrose. He says that the Big Bang does not mark the beginning, but merely the latest of a series of Big Bangs providing an ever-renewable possible reality, each very different from the previous version. He is of the view that past Big Bangs left an imprint, a kind of fossilised energy pattern that can be detected and analysed. In his version, the universe continues to expand, and all particles of matter become rarefied and lose their mass and hence their individual identities. If all particles become massless, they transform into light, which is a timeless and spaceless unified entity, and the universe would look to them to be infinitely small. This infinitely small universe, the singular-

2 - The View of Origins

ity, is what undergoes a Big Bang, and so on.

From the dawn of time, humans have searched for certainty in the universe. The celestial motions, in contrast to the earthly turbulent motions of life, seem to proceed with serene certainty. They realised that the profound message of the definite motion of the stars is that certain knowledge of the universe is possible. By tracking the planets they learned that their motion was not random but has a pattern. There is order in heaven, and therefore it was the domain of the celestial beings and was made of heavenly materials that followed a certain order, unlike the earthly world of capricious appearance. The goal was finding the physical laws, the internal logic that governs the entire universe, in order to find the order beyond immediate experience.

Rational science presumes that the universe is governed by laws that can be known by us but are independent of our thoughts and feelings. The assumed existence of this cosmic code is the faith that moves natural science. Natural science sees in that code the eternal structure of reality written into the very substance of the universe. This is the classical view of reality.

The character of physical laws, or patterns governing the forms, follows general principles. The first principle is invariance. It states that there are things that don't change things that are invariant. The question that follows therefore is: why is it reasonable to suppose that all the apparent changes in the world are subject to invariant laws? The crucial insight of the age of reason was to separate conceptually the actual state of the world of form from the invisible laws that describe how such a state changes, laws that can be quite simple. The core idea is that beyond the changing world of the many is a changeless one. The modern idea of invariance is a consequence of symmetry.

Symmetry, in appearance or form, implies invariance. Translational invariance in space, that is, motion of an object without seeing the difference and without changing its state, implies that the law applies to events regardless of their location in space. This also applies to time translational invariance. The law is not subject to changes in time. This crucial breakthrough was discovered by the mathematician Emmy Noether: that for every symmetry in physics, there is a corresponding conservation law. Conservation of energy, for example, states that for a closed system the sum total of all energy, heat, motion and so on, is invariant, which is related to time translational symmetry. The unchanging nature of physical laws in time logically require conservation of energy. The history of physics is the story of the search for symmetries, implying the search and discovery of the invariant conservation laws.

The second principle is universality and simplicity, meaning the same laws governing the motion of the stars also apply to the motion of objects on Earth. The law of gravity is universal. All complexity arises in a logical fashion from a few elemental but profound concepts.

The third principle is completeness. The physicists' ultimate goal is to have a unified theory of all physics. Electricity and magnetism, once seen as separate forces, became unified in Maxwell's electromagnetic theory. Space and time are unified in Einstein's relativity theory. Quantum field theory unified the strong nuclear force and the electromagnetic and weak forces inside the atom. A complete theory is the dream of the age of reason.

An important feature of any scientific theory is not that the conclusions are provable, but rather that they must be disprovable. A theory may be founded on very general laws, but from those laws we must be able to deduce specific properties of the world. Only specific, unambiguous predictions can be tested. A theory cannot be right in general unless it can also be wrong specifically. To be falsifiable a theory must be logically precise and unambiguous. In order to possess that unambiguity, physics is specified in the precise language of mathematics. The physical world is quantifiable, which means we can measure and assign numbers to it. These numbers are then related by an algebraic formula that expresses a law of nature imposing constraints or boundaries on the world. Classical physics believed that all of nature could be described by mathematics. In quantum theory, however, the idea of a mathematical description of all nature broke down. Individual quantum events are not subject to any mathematical-physical law; only the distribution of these events

2 - The View of Origins

can be so described. Only the averages of many observations are subject to the laws of quantum theory. At the level of the individual subatomic particle, the laws of physics are not deterministic but statistical, not subject to a precise mathematical description.

The search for physical laws has not been an entirely objective activity independent of our subjective, individual psychological and collective cultural worldview, which often determines the direction of the inquiry. We cannot underestimate the role of intuition and imagination in science. In the real world, the problem is to find the problem, and asking the right questions takes imagination. Preconceived opinion is a crucial part of scientific inquiry. It is this partiality that guides the imagination to the relevant facts. Our attraction to the beautiful, what is coherent and simple, is at the heart of the human capability of rationally comprehending the material world. Beauty is in the eye of the beholder. The visual aesthetic of geometry appeals to some; to others, beauty is the abstract world of symbols. In quantum physics the aesthetic sense is conceptual. Instead of images, we have symmetries described by mathematics. The organising principle is symmetry.

The evolutionary principle in the physical world is also based on broken symmetries. The unfolding of the universe into distinctive phases is characterised by the manifestation of broken symmetries that form the boundaries of the evolving universe.

Science is one of the deepest expressions of the human desire to realise the vision of infinite knowledge, the search for simplicity, order, and the ultimate building blocks from which the universe is made. The visible world is neither spirit nor matter. It is the invisible organisation of energy manifested in patterns or forms. A prime driver of the developments in physics is the uncovering of symmetry or beauty in the metaphysical equations.

IMAGINATION

Imaginal, or thought, experiments are tests of hypothesis that take place in the imagination, because such experiments are not possible to perform in the laboratory or the 'real world'. Imaginal science appears throughout history as allegories, of which the most famous is Plato's allegory of the cave, in which he suggest that humans live in the visible world of change and uncertainty, which is only a manifestation of the perfect realm of forms. The greatest modern proponent of imaginal science is Albert Einstein. His earliest passion was the nature of light. He asked himself what a light wave would look like if he could travel alongside it at the speed of light. He could not perform the experiment directly. He had to rely on principles of symmetry, logic, and mathematics. After 10 years he arrived at the *special theory of relativity*. He followed this with another imaginal experiment, and asked whether he could tell the difference between the effects of gravity or acceleration if he were enclosed in a box that was accelerating. This led to the most beautiful theory in physics: the *theory of general relativity*.

The twentieth century had relied more and more on imaginal physics to drive its development, as higher and higher energies are probed with smaller and smaller distances, especially when trying to understand the new views of reality that are not visualisable and are without any experimental evidence. For some 400 years, physics has been led by experiments, but this is no longer the case with the latest ideas from string theory and other grand unification theories. Although scientific history from Pythagoras to string theory has been inspired by ideas of symmetry, beauty and perfection, they have often been stumbling blocks. Certain ideas about perfect numbers or perfect geometries influenced the theories of the Cosmos. For example, it was believed that the movement of the heavenly bodies should be circular in shape, because the circle was believed to be perfect. But how do we define or know what perfection is? Absolute perfection is beyond us; we can only conceive of relative perfections that satisfy a limited set of criteria according to a certain point of view. The Greeks considered symmetry to be the unifying principle. This continues to a large degree in modern science.

> *The principle of science, the definition, almost, is the following: The test of all knowledge is experiment. Experiment is the sole*

2 - The View of Origins

judge of scientific 'truth.' But what is the source of knowledge? Where do the laws that are to be tested come from? Experiment, itself, helps to produce these laws, in the sense that it gives us hints. But also needed is imagination to create from these hints the great generalizations—to guess at the wonderful, simple, but very strange patterns beneath them all, and then to experiment to check again whether we have made the right guess. This imagining process is so difficult that there is a division of labor in physics: there are theoretical physicists who imagine, deduce, and guess at new laws, but do not experiment; and then there are experimental physicists who experiment, imagine, deduce, and guess.
—Richard Feynman

3 - The View of Light

Allah is the Light of the heavens and the earth; the parable of His Light is as a niche wherein is a lamp, the lamp in a glass, the glass as it were a glittering star kindled from a Blessed Tree, an olive that is neither of the East nor of the West whose oil well-nigh would shine, even if no fire touched it; Light upon Light; Allah guides to His Light whom He will. And Allah strikes parables for mankind, and God has knowledge of everything.
—Qur'an 24.35

Your eye has not strength enough to gaze at the burning sun, but you can see its burning light by watching its reflection mirrored in the water.
So the reflection of Absolute Being can be viewed in the mirror of Non-Being, for nonexistence, being opposite Reality, instantly catches its reflection.
Know the world from end to end is a mirror; in each atom a hundred suns are concealed.
If you pierce the heart of a single drop of water, from it will flow a hundred clear oceans; if you look intently at each speck of dust, in it you will see a thousand beings.
A gnat in its limbs is like an elephant; in name a drop of water resembles the Nile.
In the heart of a barleycorn is stored a hundred harvests. Within a millet-seed a world exists. In an insects wing is an ocean of life. A heaven is concealed in the pupil of an eye.
The core at the center of the heart is small, yet the Lord of both worlds will enter there.
—Mahmud Shabistari

A New World

By the end of the nineteenth century, a new worldview would begin to emerge. It would start with two mysteries or anomalies. The first would be the discovery that something was missing in the mechanical picture of light, that light waves travelled without any substance to wave in. The second would be the realisation that the colours of light from any hot glowing material, such as the filament of a light bulb, could not be explained by the mechanical movement or vibrations of that material. With these anomalies regarding the behaviour of light, quantum mechanics would begin to break the grounds of the age of certainty.

Throughout the first half of the nineteenth century, many scientists began to accept the idea that heat and light were at least qualitatively identical. According to Newton, light consisted of tiny particles that were able to move through the vacuum of space. Light, therefore, was defined as a substance. Heat, too, was considered a substance. However, Thomas Young discovered that light particles can somehow interfere with each other. He observed interference patterns that can only be produced by waves, not particles. The patterns were a result of the blending of light waves into each other. There was only one problem: waves must move through something but they don't travel in a vacuum. Thus it was thought that light waves must wave in some invisible substance called ether that filled all of space.

Another important discovery was made by Michael Faraday, namely, that electricity could be turned into magnetism and back again. This interchange, called electromagnetism, led to the theoretical discovery of electromagnetic waves by James Clerk Maxwell. He discovered that these electromagnetic waves move at the speed of light.

Maxwell's 'electromagnetic theory' embodied the notion that things we can measure directly, such as mechanical force, are merely the outward manifestations of deeper processes, involving entities such as electric field strength, which are beyond our powers of visualisation. The theory encapsulated some of the more fundamental characteristics of the universe. Not only did it

3 - The View of Light

explain all known electromagnetic phenomena, it also explained light and pointed to the existence of types of radiation long before their discovery. The theory predicted that electromagnetic waves travelled at a speed equal to the ratio of the electromagnetic and electrostatic units of charge. This led to the discovery that light itself is composed of electromagnetic waves. Maxwell had great intuition in finding ways in which the natural world followed mathematical principles that are not obvious from sense experience alone, thus showing that mathematical equations can shed light on the hidden structures of reality. This had a profound influence on science from then on. He was the first to use field equations to represent physical processes. They are now the standard form used by physicists to model what goes on in the vastness of space and inside atoms.

He was also the first to use statistical methods to describe processes involving many particles, another technique that is now a standard. His equations were a fundamental departure from Newtonian mechanical theory to a more holistic field theory, where energy exists potentially everywhere, eliminating the notion of action at a distance of Newtonian physics. Field theory was the chief inspiration for Einstein's theory of relativity and played a part in the discovery of quantum theory.

This was followed by Heinrich Hertz showing experimentally that light and heat are also electromagnetic waves. But how did these waves travel? And what exactly was waving?

In 1887, Albert Michelson and Edward Morley attempted to measure the presence of the 'ether' existing between the Sun and the Earth by measuring the speed of the Earth relative to this fixed immovable 'ether'. The experiment was thought to be a failure because it did not detect the 'ether'. By exploring the depths of matter and energy, by analysing things both mathematically and experimentally, physicists would find that they had to abandon the Newtonian continuous mechanical picture of the physical world. Light waves travelled without anything to wave in, and light energy was not continuously emitted by hot substances that glowed the colours of light. It would be this discontinuity that would lead

Werner Heisenberg and Niels Bohr back to the earlier Greek picture of wholeness.

Quantum Age

In 1900 Max Planck discovered theoretically, that matter absorbed heat and emitted light discontinuously. *Discontinuously* means in lumps. Planck's idea related the energy given to the wave by the oscillating material with the frequency of that wave, which was something original in physics. The energy, either absorbed by the material or emitted as light, depended on the frequency of the light emitted. This was the beginning of the quantum age. Later, Einstein reasoned that the cause of the discontinuities in the emission and absorption of light and heat were not to be found in the oscillating bits of matter producing the heat and light. They were instead in the heat and light energy. He felt that light was not fundamentally made of waves, but tiny granules called photons. By 1911, the quantum nature of light as a wave that somehow had a particular graininess associated with it, had become acceptable, although the Newtonian classical worldview still persisted.

Quantum physics has taught us that we, the observers of reality, are at the same time the participants of reality. However, our classical worldview has preconditioned us to think objectively, to see the world as preexistent. Objectivity, however, takes its toll. The cost is your awareness of your awareness, that objectivity is only an illusion. I make a choice and an object appears, but I have lost my awareness of choosing it. When the object appears, I vanish. At the instant the object appears, I project the object's appearance out of my mind. It becomes an act of sudden 'creation'. That action of choice separated 'me' from 'it'. The picture of the object in my mind becomes the real object out there.

In the quantum world, any two points in space and time are both separate and not separate. The speed of light sets a clear upper boundary on the separability of places and times. When points are connected by signals travelling at speeds slower than the speed of light, the points are separate. When they reach the

3 - The View of Light

speed of light signals begin to lose meaning. Einstein's special theory of relativity predicts that neither space nor time 'appears' for a particle of light. This is due to the fact that the speed of light is constant. Any observer watching light as it moves from a source to a receiver would measure the light's speed to be the same. This is true even if the observer is moving relative to the source and/or the receiver, and no matter how fast the observer travels.

In proposing his theory, Einstein postulated that the speed of light was a universal constant. However fast you may be moving relative to a light beam, you will always measure the speed of light to be the same 186,000 miles per second. Even if you are moving at 99 per cent of the speed of light, light will still appear to travel past you at 186,000 miles per second.

Although this is totally counterintuitive, experiments show that it does indeed seem to be the case. This raises two difficult questions:

1. First, why is the speed always the same?
2. Second, why is light so special? When we distinguish the image of reality from the underlying reality, the apparent constancy of the speed of light takes on a very different nature.

According to Einstein, as an observer's speed increases, time slows down, and space (in the direction of motion) contracts. At the speed of light, time has slowed to a standstill and space contracted to a point. Although no object with mass can ever attain the speed of light, if it were to do so, it would then have infinite mass. From light's point of view light itself has travelled no distance, and has taken no time to do so.

This reflects a unique property of light. In the space-time continuum there is no separation between the emission of a light ray and its absorption. What Einstein called the 'space-time interval' between the two ends of a light ray is always zero.

However, when we perceive the world from our human frame of reference, we do indeed observe a separation between the two ends of the light beam, with the exact amount of separation depending upon our speed. We could say the act of perception 'stretches out' the zero interval, and divides it into a certain amount of space and a certain amount of time. Because the total interval remains zero, the amount of space created exactly balances the amount of time created. For every 186,000 miles of space, we 'create' 1 second of time.

What we conceive of as the speed of light is actually something completely different. From light's point of view and not our matter-bound mode of experience, light travels no distance in no time, and therefore has no need of speed. What we take to be the speed of light is actually the ratio in which space and time are created in our image of reality. It is this ratio that is fixed, and this is why in the phenomenal world the apparent speed of light is fixed.

The constancy of the speed of light implies that space and time are relative quantities. Moving clocks tick slower and moving rods shrink. The faster an object moves in relation to the observer, the slower its clock runs and the shorter it becomes. The limit to all this relativity is the speed of light. Beyond the speed of light, an object or a consciousness would be completely free of the shackles of space and time. It could 'drop in' at any time, past or future. The universe is not just a collection of separate points. It is what it is according to the observer and what he or she does. By identifying with the 'wholeness' of the world, the observer 'becomes' the observed. He is what he sees.

Although all we ever see is light, paradoxically, we never know light directly. The light that strikes the eye is known only through the energy it releases. This energy is translated into a visual image in the mind, and that image seems to be composed of light—but that light is a quality of mind. We never actually know the light itself.

Conscious Light

Physics, like spirituality, suggests that in the beginning there is light, for light underlies every process in the present moment. Any exchange of energy between any two atoms in the universe

3 - The View of Light

involves the exchange of photons. Every interaction in the material world is mediated by light. In this way, light penetrates and interconnects the entire cosmos. Light is synonymous with the absolute in physics. Light lies beyond the manifest world of matter, shape and form, beyond both space and time. Consciousness is often spoken of as the inner light. Those who have awakened to the truth about reality are called illumined or enlightened, and they describe their experiences in terms of light.

> *Gleaming into the unseen, I gazed at it continually, until the time came when I had wholly become that light.*
> —*Abu 'l-Hasayn al-Nuri*

Physical light has no mass and is not part of the material world; the same is true of consciousness. Light seems, in some way, fundamental to the universe in that its values are absolute, universal constants. The light of consciousness is likewise fundamental; without it there would be no experience.

Do physical reality and the reality of the mind share the same common ground, a ground whose essence is light? We now begin to see just how close the parallels are between the light of physics and the light of consciousness: both are beyond the material world, both seem to lie beyond space and time, both seem intrinsically unknowable, and both are absolutes. Every photon of light is an identical quantum of action, and the foundation of every interaction in the universe. The light of consciousness is likewise absolute and invariant. It is the source of every quality that we ever experience and its essential nature is the same for everyone. Because it is beyond all attributes and identifying characteristics, there is no way to distinguish the light of consciousness in any human being. In this sense, we are all the same consciousness and we all know the same inner self.

Gnostics have spoken of this inner light as the Divine Light, the Cosmic Light, the Light of Light, the Eternal Light that shines in every heart. The Uncreated Light from which all creation takes form. It is the light of consciousness shining at the core of every form in the cosmos, the Pure Consciousness that is the very essence of self.

> *Time and space are but physiological colors which the eye makes, but the Soul is light.*
> —*Ralph Waldo Emerson*

> *'I' and 'you' are but the lattices, in the niches of a lamp, through which the One Light shines. 'I' and 'you' are the veil between heaven and earth; lift this veil and you will see no longer the bonds of sects and creeds. When 'I' and 'you' do not exist, what is mosque, what is synagogue? What is the Temple of Fire?*
> —*Mahmud Shabistari*

4 - The View of Time and Space

It is He who created for you all that is in the earth, then He ascended Himself to heaven and leveled the seven heavens; and He has knowledge of everything.
—Qur'an 2.29

In physics the distinction between past, present and future is only a stubbornly persistent illusion.
—Albert Einstein

Sacred Geometry

The world that we experience is one of infinite possible worlds with countless varieties and complexities, a multidimensional world that contains no straight lines or completely regular shapes, where things do not happen in sequences, but all together, a world where, as modern physics tells us, even empty space is curved. It is clear that our abstract system of conceptual thinking can never describe or understand this reality completely. In thinking about the world, we are faced with the same kind of problem as the cartographer who tries to cover the curved face of the Earth with a sequence of plane maps. We can only expect an approximate representation of reality from such a procedure, and all rational knowledge is therefore necessarily limited.

The ancient worldview is essentially that of a timeless order in which each thing has its proper place. Aristotle describes an eternal order of increasing perfection, going from earthly matter to heavenly matter. By the Middle Ages, this view found its eternal basis in the order of religion and philosophy, from which laws, morals and ethics, which regulated the temporal concerns of society, had their grounds.

After the Middle Ages, this order began to give rise to the new secular order in which everything was regarded as being subject to the flux of time. Motion was reduced to a mechanical process that had no ultimate goal and was therefore going nowhere in particular. This secular order was atomistic in nature, and as a result the individual came to assume a more prominent role in society.

In Newton's mechanics, the order of space and time was accepted as absolute and in this sense, therefore, something remained from Aristotle's order. However, with Einstein, this order changed. In the theory of relativity it was shown that the flow of time depends on the speed of the observer. Past, present and future could not be maintained in the same absolute sense as in Newton's view.

By the end of the nineteenth century, physics was dominated by the classical deterministic worldview, which had produced the great achievements of the theory of heat and Maxwell's electromagnetic theory. A major problem that remained was how to deduce the laws of mechanical motion of electrically charged particles from the electromagnetic theory.

Radioactivity, the spontaneous emission of particles and rays from specific materials, was a major puzzle. These were the first signs that led to the end of the domination of classical physics.

In those days positivism was dominant, which states that all physical theory must come only from direct experimental experience, all ideas that cannot be tested experimentally must be abandoned. At that time the existence of atoms was only a hypothesis without any experimental confirmation.

As already previously mentioned, the first crucial idea in quantum theory came from Planck in 1900. Classical physics is built on the idea that all physical phenomena are continuous and could take any value. However, the basic idea of Planck's hypothesis is that the continuous worldview must be replaced by a discontinuous, or discrete one. Due to the fact that the discrete-

4 - The View of Time and Space

ness of physical quantities is very small, their discreteness is not perceptible to our senses. The continuous nature of our classical view is an illusion. This idea was one of the great leaps of the rational imagination, and represents a breakthrough in the symmetry that ushered in a new phase of understanding the universe.

In 1905, Einstein published three papers that began the revolution in physics of the twentieth century. The first paper, on statistical mechanics, confirmed the existence of atoms as observed in the so-called Brownian motion, explaining that the movement of pollen grains in liquid was due to atoms bouncing off the grains.

The second paper was on the photoelectric effect, explaining that light shining on a specific metal produces electric current. Einstein made use of Planck's quantum hypothesis and made the radical assumption that light itself was quantised into particles, later called photons, little packets of energy. In classical physics, light was thought of as a wavelike phenomenon in accordance with the view of nature as a continuum. Experimental confirmation of the photon did not come until 1923 by Arthur Compton, who confirmed the scattering of photons by electrons.

The third paper was on special relativity, which changed our view of space and time. Einstein postulated that it was impossible to determine absolute uniform motion. You can only determine uniform motion by comparing your motion relative to another object. He also confirmed the absolute speed of light, which makes its speed qualitatively different from the speed of anything else. It is the interplay between the relativity of motion for all objects and the absoluteness of the speed of light that is at the root of all the unfamiliar features or experiences of the world, according to special relativity. He deduced that space shrinks with motion, approaching zero at the speed of light. Time also slows down for a moving object. At the speed of light, time stands still. Absolute space and time were abolished.

In a follow-up paper the same year, he presented the famous formula $E = mc^2$, showing that energy and mass are equivalent, whereas it had previously been thought that the quantities were distinct and that these quantities were conserved. Mass and energy are different manifestations of the same thing. They only appear as distinct. Time and space, matter and energy are not absolute, invariant quantities. They are relative, observer-dependent quantities.

In 1915 Einstein completed his greatest work: the theory of general relativity, which addressed accelerated or non-uniform motion where the speed of objects is changing or a change in directions occurs. The first main idea is that it is impossible to distinguish the experience of non-uniform motion from the effect of gravity, like the experience of an ascending lift. This is called the principle of equivalence, the equivalence of non-uniform motion and gravity. Einstein discovered the laws relating to space and time as seen by two observers moving non-uniformly. He intuited the results before finding the mathematical rules to express them. The creation of general relativity offers an example of physics utilising existing mathematical tools to find the right language to express intuitions. The mathematical tools in this case was the geometry of curved space, known as Riemannian geometry. Our normal flat, non-curved geometry of everyday experience is called Euclidean geometry.

Einstein used the three-dimensional curvature of space to describe gravity, including time, which made four dimensions. We cannot visualise such a universe of four-dimensional space-time. Einstein saw that gravity was a superfluous concept in that there is no such thing as a 'gravitational force'. What happens is that any mass curves the space-time near it, altering its geometry. He basically discovered that gravity is geometry. It is the curvature of space-time, replacing the old Newtonian idea that matter attracts other matter across absolute space and time. This is the central conclusion of general relativity. Einstein proposed three experiments to test his theory. These were:

1. A slight bending of light in the gravitational field of the sun.
2. A small shift in the orbit of the planet Mercury, and
3. Clocks should run slower in a gravity field.

4 - The View of Time and Space

In 1991 the first test was confirmed during an eclipse of the Sun. After 200 years, Newton's law of gravitation was overthrown. The two other tests were confirmed with the use of modern technology to measure the effects of gravity on the orbit of Mercury and the slowing down of time in a gravitational field.

Einstein revealed that space and time are not absolutes. They vary according to the motion of the observer. Time and space stretch and compress according to the motion of a localised observer. This is almost impossible for us to conceive. Yet numerous experiments have shown it to be true. It is our commonsense notions of space and time that are wrong. They are constructs in the mind and do not perfectly model what is out there. Space and time have fallen from their absolute status. They are both created through the act of perception and so belong to the relative world of experience. This is not to imply that they are not fundamental to our experience. They are the dimensional framework within which we structure our mental image of the world. But we deceive ourselves when we assume that they are also fundamental to the underlying reality.

Mindscapes

The philosopher Immanuel Kant foresaw that space and time are a frame of reference in which the mind constructs its experience some 100 years before Einstein. They are built into the perceiving process, and we cannot but think in terms of space and time. But they are not aspects of the objective reality. That reality, according to Einstein, is something else, what he called space-time. When observed, space-time appears as a certain amount of space and a certain amount of time. However, the amount of which is perceived as space and the amount of which is perceived as time are not fixed; they are dependent upon the motion of the observer.

If space, time and matter have no absolute objective status, what about energy? Energy is defined as the potential to do work, that is, to create change. Energy comes in many different forms—potential energy, kinetic energy, chemical energy, electrical energy, heat energy, radiation energy—yet we never measure energy as such, only the changes that we attribute to energy.

Energy is often said to be a fundamental quality of the cosmos, but that too turns out to be a mistake. According to the special theory of relativity, energy and mass are interchangeable, related by Einstein's famous equation, $E = mc^2$. Observers travelling at different speeds will differ in their measurements of how much energy an object has.

Quantum theory offers further clues as to the nature of energy. The quantum is commonly called a quantum of energy, the smallest possible unit of energy. But that is not strictly correct. The quantum is actually a quantum of action. What is action? It is another physical quantity like distance, velocity, momentum, and force.

The amount of action in a quantum is exceedingly small, about 0.000000000000000000000000000662607 erg.sec, *erg* being a unit of energy. It is considered to be one of the constants of nature, more fundamental than space, time, matter or energy. The zero-point field is not, therefore, a potential energy field. It is a potential quantum field, a field of potential action. A photon is a single quantum of light, but the energy associated with a photon varies enormously. A gamma-ray photon, for example, packs trillions of times more energy than a radiowave photon. But each and every photon, each and every quantum, is an identical unit of action.

When the photon is absorbed by the retina of the eye, it manifests as a certain amount of energy, measured by the amount of change it is capable of creating. This change is what is conveyed to the brain and then interpreted as colour. The amount of change, or energy, is dependent upon the frequency of the underlying electromagnetic field, which is why we see different colours corresponding to different frequencies of light.

Frequency is another model taken from experience and then imagined to apply to the photon. It is most unlikely that a photon has frequency as we think of it. Indeed, even the idea of a photon is another example of how we have projected our experience on to the external world. We experience particles so we imagine that

4 - The View of Time and Space

light might be a particle. We also have the experience of waves, so we imagine light as a wave. Sometimes light seems to fit one description, other times another. Light is neither strictly a wave nor a particle.

Our whole experience is a construction in the mind, a form appearing in consciousness. These mental forms are composed not of physical substance but of 'mind stuff'. What appear to us as fundamental dimensions and attributes of the physical world space, time, matter and energy—are but the fundamental dimensions and attributes of the forms appearing in consciousness.

The theory of general relativity implies the existence of gravity waves, vibrations of the curvature of space-time that propagate at the speed of light. General relativity provided the basis for cosmology, the study of the entire universe. Physicist Alexander Friedmann was the first to apply Einstein's equations to the entire universe.

In 1922 Friedmann found that the solution to the equations implied that the universe was not static; it had to be changing, expanding or contracting in time. He showed that if the density of the galaxies was below a critical value, then the universe was open and would continue to expand forever, and, in contrast, if the density was above a critical value, then the universe would be closed and would eventually contract. The evidence we have to date is that the universe is open. Hubble, an astronomer, discovered that the universe is indeed expanding like a gigantic explosion, and is evolving. The theory of general relativity therefore represented the fulfilment of the classical deterministic worldview. It was an improvement of Newtonian physics, but the principles were not altered.

Fundamentally, Einstein did not rely on observation, experimentation or standard rational deductive methods to come up with his theory. He had to make a leap to a conceptual abstract absolute postulate, such as the equivalence principle. Then he used the postulate to deduce specific theoretical results that can be experimentally tested. The absolute postulate transcends experience: it comes from intuition. A great deal of creative work in science proceeds by this method, which places intuition at the very step, a non-rational, but verifiable aspect of scientific creativity.

This was the most radical change in the notion of order since Isaac Newton and quantum mechanics. It was no longer possible to define position and momentum (speed) simultaneously, nor could an unambiguous notion of a particle's path be maintained. The new system depended on the more abstract idea of symmetries, quantum states and energy levels. The quantum-mechanical idea of order contradicts the perceived space time order because Heisenberg's uncertainty principle made a detailed ordering of space and time impossible. When you apply quantum theory to general relativity at very short distances like 10^{-33} centimetres, the notion of the order of space and time breaks down. Order is a dynamic process that involves subject, object, and the cycle of perception-communication that unites and relates them.

The whole transformation from the old eternal order has brought in its wake a movement away from the absolute, and toward the idea that things are inherently relative and dependent on conditions and contexts. Newton attempted to formulate universal laws that were assumed to be eternally valid, and therefore appealed to something that lay beyond time. However, these laws were eventually found to hold true only under certain limited conditions and could not be eternal. Even the theories of relativity and quantum mechanics that replaced the Newtonian worldview are questionable. The phenomena of 'black holes', which as we know, are singularities in the fabric of space-time within which all the known laws of physics, including relativity and quantum theory, break down, and basic structures, such as elementary particles, cease to exist. This reflects that was mistakenly directed to the outer universe: the contents of consciousness rather than the ground of consciousness itself.

From the concept of space–time arise interdependent counterparts such as subject and object, positive and negative, yin and yang, alternating in time and separate in space. Neither element of any pair of opposites or complementaries has any but a conceptual existence, and their resolution returns them to their

4 - The View of Time and Space

source. 'Superimposed', each member of each pair of concepts annuls the other, and the result phenomenally is blank, and noumenally is non-being or non-manifestation, which is total absence as phenomenon, and total presence as noumenon. That is the resolution of Duality. —Wei Wu Wei

ORIENTATIONS

A physical sense of the direction of time comes from a property of the second law of thermodynamics which is called entropy. It is a measure of how disorganised, random-like in appearance a physical system is, and is also an emergent macroscopic property. The increase of entropy in a closed system is the second law of thermodynamics. The *'law of entropy increase'* is consistent because a highly organised configuration is improbable, compared to a disorganised one, and it is more likely for a state of nature to go from an improbable configuration to a highly probable one.

From the microscopic individual particle point of view the situation is entirely different. There is equal probability that a particle can go either way. Order and disorder have meaning only at the macroscopic level. The law makes sense only if we have a large number of particles so that we can speak of a probability distribution, which is an averaging of the motion of many particles.

The microscopic description of a physical system in terms of the motion of individual particles is given by Newton's laws of motion. These laws make no distinction between past and future. From the standpoint of the microscopic world, time can literally have either direction. An atom knows nothing about ageing; it is how atoms and molecules are organised that determines age. Irreversible time, ageing, and the rotting of fruit are all illusions from the point of view of microphysics. However, the law of entropy increase gives time an arrow, a direction that distinguishes the past and future.

The microscopic laws are therefore said to be time-reversal invariant, and the macroscopic laws, such as the law of entropy, increase are not. It is therefore impossible to derive the second law of thermodynamics, which is a law for the macroscopic variable entropy, from the laws of Newton's mechanics, meaning that emergent properties are not reducible to lower layers.

It is we who recognise the pattern and it is we who impose the macroscopic description of physical reality, a reality that does not apply to the micro-world. We can draw a line between the micro-world and the macro-world of human experience; they are qualitatively distinct descriptions of material reality.

The micro-world is indifferent to success or failure, selfishness or altruism. Nature has however, produced organisms that know these differences and respond to patterns that are meaningless from the point of view of the micro-world. The human world, although supported by the micro-world, exists for its own sake. Civilisation reflects a pattern of human existence that is consistent with the fundamental laws of the micro-world but cannot be derived from them.

Nature knows nothing of imperfection. Imperfection is a human perception. Inasmuch as we are part of nature, we are perfect. It is our humanity worldview that is imperfect. Ironically, because of this capacity to perceive imperfection and error, we are free beings in essence.

> *The reason why people cannot stop time quickly is that they are looking forward to something. They have shackled themselves to their houses, their jobs, their situations. However, since non-time is already inherent in us, we are already free—but we do not know it. What, then, is freedom? It is knowledge, the realization that we are never separate from the non-time Reality. The knowledge that there is one Reality encompassing everything is the ultimate freedom.*
> —Shaykh Fadhlala Haeri

From the first moments of the Big Bang, the energy was so great that the four forces or interactions of gravitation, electromagnetic, weak nuclear and strong nuclear were unified as one highly symmetrical interaction. As the universe expanded and cooled down, the perfect symmetry began to break. First, gravity was distinguished from the other interactions, and then the strong, weak and electromagnetic interactions became apparent, manifesting symmetry breaking. The universe can be viewed as a hierarchy of symmetry breaking, from simple perfect symmetry to complex patterns of broken symmetries. Similarly, as we shall see later, in a biological context, a cell starts as unit that divides itself, undergoing a highly symmetrical process of division.

> *Thought is time. Thought is born of experience and knowledge, which are inseparable from time and the past. Time is the psychological enemy of man. Our action is based on knowledge and therefore time, so man is always a slave to the past. Thought is ever limited and so we live in constant conflict and struggle. There is no psychological evolution. When man becomes aware of the movement of his own thoughts, he will see the division between the thinker and thought, the observer and the observed, the experiencer and the experience. He will discover that this division is an illusion. Then only is there pure observation which is insight without any shadow of the past or of time. This timeless insight brings about a deep, radical mutation in the mind. Total negation is the essence of the positive. When there is negation of all those things that thought has brought about psychologically, only then is there love, which is compassion and intelligence.*
> —J.Krishnamurti

5 - The View of Matter and Energy

And you see the mountains, thinking them rigid, while they will pass as the passing of clouds. The work of Allah, who perfected all things. Indeed, He is acquainted with that which you do.
—*Qur'an 27.88*

And when Moses came to Our appointed time and his Lord spoke to him, he said, 'Oh my Lord, show me, that I may look upon Thee!' Said He, 'Thou shalt not see Me; but behold the mountain if it stays fast in its place, then thou shalt see Me.' And when his Lord disclosed Himself to the mountain, He made it crumble to dust, and Moses fell down thunderstruck.
—*Qur'an 7.143*

Primal Uncertainty

The discovery of indeterminism in the quantum reality opened the door to a new vision of nature. The predictions of quantum theory are for the distributions of events, not individual events. Probability distributions are causally determined and not specific events. Niels Bohr came up with the primary insight into the meaning of quantum theory. He postulated the principle of complementarity. Bohr emphasised that in asking a question about nature, we must also specify the experimental apparatus used to determine the answer. The very act of observation changes the state of the observed. Particles and waves are cthe principle of complementarity in quantum physics, meaning they exclude one another. They are different representations of the same object. We can describe the object in ways that are mutually exclusive: as wave or particle. The experimental arrangements that determine these descriptions are also mutually exclusive. The experiment and therefore the description are subject to our choice. In effect, the objective realm and the subjective realm are not independent.

Independently, Werner Heisenberg discovered the uncertainty principle, describing it in precise mathematical terms. He showed that you cannot simultaneously measure different physical properties of a particle, such as its position and momentum, with high precision. There is an inherent uncertainty in the measurement process. However, this does not apply to single measurements. It is a statement about statistical averages over many measurements. For everyday objects, the uncertainties due to quantum theory are very small; therefore, to a high degree of accuracy, the object obeys the deterministic laws of classical physics. For an electron, the quantum of uncertainties completely dominates. Together the complementarity and the uncertainty principles came to be known as the *Copenhagen interpretation* of quantum mechanics, which renounced determinism and the objectivity of the classical realm.

In summary, the Copenhagen interpretation of the quantum theory rejected determinism, accepting instead the statistical nature of reality, and it rejected objectivity, accepting instead that material reality depends in part on how we choose to observe it. The essence of this interpretation is that the world must be actually observed to be objective. With the new quantum theory, the basis for the periodic table of chemical elements, the nature of the chemical bond and molecular chemistry became understood. These new developments gave rise to modern quantum chemistry. This was followed by molecular biology, which culminated in the discovery of the molecular structure of DNA, the physical basis for organic reproduction.

In 1935 Einstein, Nathan Rosen and Boris Podolsky uncovered a paradox suggesting that quantum theory is incomplete. Einstein's view was that the Copenhagen interpretation and objective reality were incompatible. He was right, but there was no

5 - The View of Matter and Energy

paradox. The main objection was that quantum theory violated local causality, which is a sacred principle in classical science, in that distant events cannot instantaneously influence local objects without mediation.

Classical physics asserts that whatever influences an object is either due to local changes in the state of the object itself or due to energy being transmitted through space-time. Quantum theory implies instant action-at-a-distance effects between two particles across space-time, which is impossible according to classical physics, because mediation is restricted by the speed of light. However this is based on the assumption of the objective reality of these particles. Quantum theory states that particles have no objective existence without being measured; therefore, it is impossible to say anything about the properties of the second particle, without actually measuring them, even if the thought experiment actually implies so, but that is a classical view, not a quantum one.

In 1965 John Stewart Bell's experiment showed that the incompleteness envisioned by Einstein was not possible. There were only two physical interpretations according to Bell: Either the world was non-objective and did not exist in a definite state, or it was non-local with instantaneous action-at-a-distance effects. Bell addressed the question of hidden variables, which specify additional information about the state of the world. Without them quantum theory remains incomplete. Bell derived a mathematical formula: an inequality that can be tested experimentally. Up-to-date experimental confirmation of this formula was carried out many times and indeed confirmed that the assumption of local causality was violated and that there are no hidden variables.

The results of Bell's experiments may imply that all parts of the universe are instantaneously interconnected; or the existence of communications faster than the speed of light. However, these assumptions are misleading and confuse the classical worldview with the quantum worldview. They assume that quantum properties exist in a definite state and that they can be altered from a distance without being measured. If we try to verify the state of a photon, for example, we find that it is not possible without altering its state. The act of measurement itself alters the initial conditions of the experiment, such that it is impossible to conclude that non-local influences exist.

To explore the micro-world of particle physics, scientists required huge instruments called accelerators. According to quantum theory, every quantum particle can be thought of as a little packet of matter wave with a particular wavelength, which is inversely proportional to its speed. The faster the particle moves, the shorter its wavelength.

A high-energy accelerator is a microscope that uses beams of particles with wavelengths smaller than the objects that can be observed. The wavelength of the particles in a beam is the critical value in determining the size of the smallest objects that can be seen using that beam. To detect smaller and smaller objects, shorter and shorter wavelengths are required. The only way to create these short wavelengths is to accelerate them up to very high speed, and that is the purpose of high-energy accelerators. Such accelerators are called matter microscopes. In an ordinary microscope, the beams consist of light photons and optical lenses to focus the light. Photons have wavelengths much larger than the objects in the nuclear world, and therefore are not suitable for that purpose. On a smaller scale, an electron microscope, which uses electron beams and magnetic lenses that have much smaller wavelengths, can show objects at the level of molecules.

The sub-nuclear world revealed new forms of particles collectively called *hadrons*. Before that, the nucleus consisted of protons and neutrons, with a particle called the *pion*, which served as the 'glue' to hold together the protons and neutrons in the nucleus. The number of hadrons discovered was very large. Physicists speculated that there were an infinite number of them. Of all the fundamental particles, only the proton, electron, photon and neutrino are observed to be stable. All other particles eventually disintegrate into one of the stable types. The hadrons represent a new level of reality that seemed endless.

The problem was how to interpret that level and what it means? One possibility is that there are endless levels each

5 - The View of Matter and Energy

forming whole/parts (holons); that there are no truly elementary particles; and that there are indefinite levels. Another possibility is that there has to be a level that cannot be subdivided and is therefore the ground of physical existence. The third possibility is given the name 'bootstrap', which is a level that is both elementary and composite, made out of particles of the same kind. Each time they are divided, they produce the same kind of particles.

In the 1960s Murray Gellman discovered that hadrons organised themselves into classes, which he called the 'eightfold way', based on a mathematical symmetry, in which he deduced that hadrons were made of even smaller particles called *'quarks'*.

Only three types of quarks—'up', 'down' and 'strange', as well as their anti-quark counterparts, which were orbiting around each other, were needed to make up all the hadrons. Because the quarks could orbit in an infinite variety of configurations, there were an infinite number of hadrons. Quarks inside the hadron also exist in orbits: thus all of these combinations of energy levels can produce an infinite number of hadrons. In 1974 a fourth type was discovered, called *Charm*, followed by a fifth called *Bottom*. Is there a 'Top' maybe!!! Quarks do not exist individually. They only exist when they are bound together in the form of hadrons. Quantum chromodynamics is the theory that describes the dynamics of quarks.

Experiments followed using a new accelerator technology, that confirmed the existence of quarks representing a new level of existence. These accelerators collided matter in the form of electrons with antimatter positrons. This collision produced new forms of energy at finer and finer levels of detail. Subsequently, the fourth and fifth quark types just mentioned were discovered.

In summary, the twentieth century identified five different levels of matter: molecules, atoms, nuclei, hadrons, quarks. The structure of matter at each deeper level becomes simpler.

A further set of particles known as leptons, from the Greek word meaning 'swift', was also discovered. Electrons belong to this set of particles. They exist outside the nucleus. Aside from the electron, other leptons are the neutrino, muon and tauon. In contrast with the hadrons, leptons have relatively weak interactions. The electron is bound to the nucleus by weak electromagnetic forces and is easily liberated to exist freely in the world. The electron has the lightest mass of all electrically charged quanta. Harnessing the electron is the basis for the electric and electronic technology of the modern age.

The theory of the electron began with Paul Dirac. This theory unified quantum theory and relativity theory. Dirac mathematically deduced the equation of the electron wave. First, the equation predicted the behavior of the electron in an electromagnetic field. Second, it predicted the existence of antimatter. It described the existence of the positron: a positively charged electron; its existence was discovered in cosmic rays. Later, antimatter versions of the proton and other particles were found. The electron seems to be the most stable particle with lightest charge that cannot decay into any lighter particles because there is none that can carry away its electric charge. The theory of the interaction of electrons with light is called quantum electrodynamics.

The second lepton is the muon. It is a major component of cosmic radiation at the surface of the Earth. The muon is similar to the electron except with a mass 200 times greater. It is also described by Dirac's equation, along with the anti-muon.

The third is the neutrino. Neutrinos are lighter than electrons, with no charge, and have only extremely weak interactions with the rest of matter. They are often produced in the decay remnants of other particles. For example, the muon decays an electron, a neutrino and an anti-neutrino. Only left-handed neutrinos exist (spin), violating parity conservation, meaning neutrinos have no mirror image. The tau, a fourth lepton, was also discovered; it is a heavy muon.

Quarks and leptons are considered the primary actors in the cosmos. Their interactions are mediated by a set of quantum particles called gluons. They are the 'glue' that holds everything together. Quarks, leptons and gluons and their organisation are, fundamentally, all the stuff of the universe. At the level of micro-reality, it is apparent that there are only four fundamental quantum interactions. From the weakest to the strongest they

5 - The View of Matter and Energy

are: first, the gravitational; second, weak interaction responsible for radioactivity; third, electromagnetic interaction; and, finally, strong quark-binding interaction.

The strength of the gluon-gluon interaction depends on the energy of the interacting particles. Quarks and leptons interacting at low energies experience the four distinct interactions. However, at very high energies, these forces are unified and the distinction vanishes. The four interactions may be considered to be four manifestations of the one interaction that existed in a unified state at the Big Bang. Each of the fundamental interactions has an associated gluon. The gluon associated with the electromagnetic field is called the Photon. The gluon-gluon of the gravity interaction is the graviton. Weak gluons mediate weak interactions, and coloured gluons provide the quark binding force.

Field Transformations

As previously explored, symmetry is related to invariance under transformation. It is how objects remain unchanged if they are transformed. For example, a sphere when rotated remains unchanged because it has rotational symmetry. Mathematically, these rotations can be described in terms of algebraic equations, using the so called Lie algebra, after the mathematician Sophus Lie, which resulted in a branch of mathematic called Lie group theory. All possible symmetries in various spaces with any number of dimensions were completely classified by the mathematician Élie Cartan.

In 1954, Chen Yang and Robert Mills applied these symmetries to quantum physics, which resulted in the Yang-Mills, or gauge, field theory. *Gauge* means measuring standard, in relation to which it was discovered that a new symmetry requires a new field.

The main discovery was that if the gauge symmetry remained exact, then the associated fields remained completely hidden or trapped inside other quanta. On the other hand, if the gauge symmetry is broken, then different components of the gauge field could manifest themselves very differently.

In summary, the exact Yang-Mills equations are symmetric, but the *solutions* to the equations, which describe manifested reality, are not symmetric. This idea of asymmetrical solutions to symmetrical equations is referred to as *spontaneous broken symmetry*. The hidden world is symmetric but not stable. There is an inbuilt natural tendency for action or excitation, which gives rise to broken symmetry, which means manifestation as patterns of form.

Spontaneous broken symmetry was the main idea used by Steven Weinberg and Mohammad Abdus Salam in 1967 to construct their gauge field theory of the unified electromagnetic and weak interactions. This was the paradigm for all unified field theories. The basic idea is that a spontaneously breaking symmetry gives rise to the difference between a weak nuclear interaction and the electromagnetic interaction.

In the symmetric situation, there are four equally massless gluons, but after a spontaneous breaking of symmetry, only one gluon remains massless, and this particle manifests as the photon of the electromagnetic interaction. The other gluons acquire mass. These are the weakly interacting gluons. Two of them have the same mass with opposite electric charge, and one is neutral. The differing masses of the four originally massless gluons reflect the broken symmetry. *Spontaneous* means that a choice is made to leverage one side of a symmetrical situation over another. The gluons alone could not spontaneously break the symmetry and give themselves different masses. The theory introduced another quantum called the *Higgs particle* after Peter Higgs (also independently discovered by François Englert, both received the Nobel Prize in 2013). The role of the Higgs particle is to make the choice to break the perfect symmetry. The search for the Higgs particle is currently the holy grail of quantum physics. Recently the CERN Large Hadron Collider is showing signs of detecting the Higgs particle.

This was followed by the gauge field theory of strong interactions, called quantum chromodynamics. The idea is that each quark had a new kind of charge, a 'color' charge, which gave

5 - The View of Matter and Energy

quarks the new property of 'color' symmetry. Exact symmetrical color invariance produced the rules for building hadrons out of quarks. The colored gluons are the origin of the strong interaction. The colored gluons provide the binding that traps the quarks inside the hadrons. Only hadrons, which are colourless combinations of the coloured quarks and gluons, can exist as free particles manifesting in the world.

This way we can see the symmetry rules manifesting in different levels of existence. At the electromagnetic and weak interaction level, broken symmetry manifests the photon and weak gluon, which can be observed. At the strong interaction level, which is a deeper level of symmetry, the color gauge symmetry remains intact and thus completely hidden. The quarks and their gluons cannot manifest; they are bound together into colourless hadrons.

The relationship between the quantitative factors of physics can be expressed mathematically, and physical changes can be described by means of equations. The construction of these equations is possible because fundamental physical quantities are conserved according to the principles of conservation of mass and energy, momentum, electric charge, and so forth. The total amount before and after a physical change is the same; however, form does not enter into these equations. It is not a quantity nor is it conserved. A form cannot be reduced to physical quantities. It is an emergent quality. Newtonian physics states that all causation is seen in terms of energy: the principle of movement and change. All moving things have energy—kinetic energy of moving bodies, thermal vibration, electromagnetic radiation—which causes other things to move. Static things have potential energy, that is, the tendency to move, because they are restrained by forces opposing this tendency.

Gravitational and electromagnetic as well as the nuclear forces are now explained in term of fields. Newtonian forces were supposed to arise from material bodies and spread out into space. However, fields are primary and they underlie both material bodies and the space between them. In field theories, physical phenomena are explained by a combination of fields and energy. Energy can be seen as the cause of change, but the order of change depends of the structure of the fields.

According to the second law of thermodynamics, spontaneous processes within a closed system tend toward a state of equilibrium, where initial differences in temperature, pressure, and other variables between different parts of the system tend to disappear. Entropy in a closed macroscopic system is directional; it increases and is irreversible. The increasing complexity of organisation that occurs in the evolution and development of living organisms appears to contradict the principle of increasing entropy. This confusion arises from misunderstanding the limitations of classical thermodynamics. First, it only applies to closed systems, whereas living organisms are open systems, exchanging mater and energy with their environment. Second, it deals with only the interrelations between heat and other forms of energy that affect chemical and biological structures but does not account for the existence of these structures. Third, it is not concerned with the type of order inherent in chemical and biological systems.

According to the third law of thermodynamics, at absolute zero, the entropies of all pure crystalline solids are zero. They are perfectly 'ordered' because there is no thermal agitation. All structures, simple or complex, have the same entropy. In the process of crystallisation, 'order' increases and macroscopic structures are developed, but from a thermodynamic point of view, 'order' has decreased because entropy and equilibrium have increased.

Formations

> *Life is already involved in Matter and Mind in Life because in essence Matter is a form of veiled Life, Life a form of veiled Consciousness.*
> —*Sri Aurobindo*

So, basically, energy and form are inversely related. Energy is the principle of change, but form or structure can only exist as long as it has a certain stability and resistance to change. Under cool-

5 - The View of Matter and Energy

er conditions, substances exist in a crystalline form with a high degree of regularity and order. As the temperature increases, the structure disintegrates into a liquid state with transient patterns that continually shift and change. The forces between the molecules create a surface tension that imparts simple forms to the liquids as a whole, as in spherical drops. With further increase in temperature, the liquid vaporises into a gaseous state in which the molecules become more isolated. At even higher temperatures, the molecules disintegrate into atoms, followed by the plasma state, where the atomic nuclei and electrons have broken up. And the reverse also applies: As the temperature is reduced, as it was in the beginning of the universe, more complex structures emerge with higher orders.

Biologist Rupert Sheldrake proposed the hypothesis of formative causation, where morphogenetic fields play a causal role in the development and maintenance of the forms of systems at all levels of complexity. A specific morphogenetic field is a cause of the specific form taken up by a system, along with the energy necessary to move the building blocks into place, whether atoms or molecules or any higher-order objects. The morphogenetic fields are analogous to the four known physical fields in which they are capable of ordering physical changes, even though they themselves cannot be observed directly. In some sense they are non-material and in another sense they are aspects of matter because they are known through their effects on material systems. In summary, chemical and biological systems are composed of hierarchies of morphic units (holons): a crystal contains molecules, which contain atoms, and so on. A higher morphic unit coordinates the arrangements of the parts of which it is composed. The higher field influences the lower ones.

One of the greatest scientific accomplishments of the nineteenth century was the invention of statistical mechanics by Maxwell, Ludwig Boltzmann and J. Willard Gibbs. The basic hypothesis is that all matter is made of particles, whose motion is determined by the laws of Newtonian classical mechanics.

In practice it is impossible to apply the mechanical laws in detail to each particle as in a gas, because there are so many of them. The main idea is to apply statistical methods so that the probability distribution of particle motion is determined, rather than the motion of each individual particle. The major accomplishment of statistical mechanics is the discovery of the laws of thermodynamics, which are statements about the distributions of particle motions. The pressure exerted by a gas on a surface is due to the particles hitting against that surface and transferring momentum to it. Similarly, the temperature of a gas is related to the average energy of motion of the particles. Pressure and temperature are macroscopic emergent properties related to the distribution of motion of a collection of particles. There is no concept of temperature for a single particle. Only if you have lots of particles does temperature emerge as a collective property.

Entropy, as already discussed earlier, is another macroscopic property of the laws of thermodynamics, and as we now know, it is a quantitative measure of how disorganised a physical system is. It is the key to understanding the relation between the micro-world and the world of human experience. In a closed physical system, entropy always increases and it is irreversible. A closed system will always change from a less probable configuration to a more probable configuration. This does not apply to open systems that exchange energy and therefore control the entropy as in self-organising systems, which we shall come to later. The law of entropy increase may apply to the whole universe because it may be considered as a closed system.

From the point of view of the mechanical properties of individual particles, the situation is seen entirely differently. The motion of particles is random and has no concept of direction from one system state to another. The law only makes sense for a large number of particles. A remarkable feature of the laws of thermodynamics is that they are not reducible to the laws of motion of individual particles. The laws of motion make no distinction between past and future; time can have either direction. An atom does not age. It is the organisation of a collection of atoms into molecules that determines age. Time is an emergent property of the collective. The direction of time is an illusion to the micro-world of the atom. But the law of entropy increase in time gives time an arrow, a direction that distinguishes the past from future. So, basically, it is a break in invariance, in symmetry that marks the evolutionary phase from the micro- to the macro-classical reality of space and time. It is impossible to derive the laws of an emergent phase from the previous one. It is a new, irreducible emergent reality.

Perceptual Patterns

> *Classical mechanics is not capable of integrating consciousness into science is manifest. Classical mechanics is an expression of Descartes's idea that nature is divided into two logically unrelated and non-interacting parts: mind and matter.*
> —Henry Stapp

It is important to realise the role of consciousness in the distinction between the micro-world and the macro-world. Our descriptions of reality are seen by and interpreted through the agency of human consciousness, an observer looking through a lens that can zoom into the micro-world of atoms moving according to Newton's laws. The observer cannot determine a direction of time from this micro-view, because the laws are timeless: there is no past or future. As the lens zoom out to give a macro-world view, there is less detail of the individual particles motion, but rather a collective motion, that is, an average view, giving the observer the sense of time, because this collective move is from an ordered state to a less ordered state, according to entropy. What has happened is an averaging, a losing out of microscopic information in favour of macroscopic information. It is our act of observation that created the macro-world, the classical view of reality, an act of averaging that gives a new emergent meaning that introduces the arrow of time. It is the observer who recognises the patterns, and it is the observer who imposes the classical view of reality, a reality that does not apply to the micro-world.

The micro-world and the macro-world are qualitatively different at the level of human experiences. Our body-mind experiences belong to the classical worldview, which is the distribution of micro-world events, such as pressure, temperature and time as a consequence of the irreversible law of entropy increase, which are, from the micro-world point of view, an illusion. This clearly demonstrates the evolutionary order of our experience of the world. Each new order is a discontinuous break from the previous one, with new emergent properties that cannot be reduced to its predecessor. A higher order transcends but includes the lower one. Each phase or reality is a level of conditioning applied by us to extract relevant meaningful information corresponding to the level of consciousness.

As consciousness evolves, new patterns are recognised, and new meanings are attributed to these collective distributions that cannot be seen from a lower level of consciousness. *Synchronicity* refers to the psychological phenomenon of attributing a pattern to different random events, an impulse to seek meaning to existence.

Every time we try to understand the essence of the physical aspect, we come away even more bewildered. Every idea we have ever had of the physical has proven to be wrong, and the notion of materiality seems to be a persistent illusion. But our belief in the material world is so deeply entrenched and so powerfully reinforced by our experience that we cling to our assumption that there must be some physical essence. Like the medieval astronomers who never questioned their assumption that the Earth was the centre of the universe, we never question our assumption that the external world is physical in nature.

All we can say about the universe is that it is not a uniform field. It contains distinctions of some kind, for it is these variations that are the origin of our perception of the world. If there were no variations in the field, there would be nothing to observe, nothing to experience. These variations in the field are the 'objects' of our perception. But they are not objects in the sense of a material object. They only become material objects in the mind of the observer. It appears to be a material 'thing' out there. We then assume that the physicality we experience, which seems so intrinsic to the world we know, must also be an intrinsic aspect of the external world. Even though there may be no physical basis

5 - The View of Matter and Energy

to the external world, the laws of physics still hold true. The only thing that changes is our assumption of what we are measuring. We are not measuring physical particles as such, but perturbations in the consciousness field. The laws of 'physics' become the laws governing the unfolding of a mental field, reflections of how perturbations in this field interact.

What we call an elementary particle would correspond to an elementary variation in the field. We might better call it an elementary entity rather than particle. Elementary entities are organised into atoms, molecules and cells, just as in the current paradigm. The difference is that we no longer have to think of consciousness sensing matter, but rather that consciousness is sensing consciousness directly. Interaction can be thought of as perception, the perception of one region in the mind-field by another. In the current view every interaction is mediated by a quantum of action (an interaction). In this alternative view, the smallest item would be a unit of perception, a unit of experience. It would be a quantum of consciousness.

The hard question of how insentient matter could ever give rise to conscious experience is now turned inside out. There is no insentient matter apart from that appearing in the mind. The question now becomes: How does the mind take on all these qualities that we experience, including that of matter? That question has been answered by direct awareness by turning the light of consciousness in upon itself, and observing the nature of mind first hand. Those who have chosen this path are the great prophets, Sufis, seers, saints, who are found throughout human history. Despite the differences in time and culture, they have come to remarkably similar conclusions. These conclusions do not, however, make much sense to the contemporary mind.

However, if we are able to see it from the point of view of contemplative personal consciousness that is able to witness the arising of mental phenomena, and hence of our whole world, it makes much more sense. Every experience, everything we ever know, is taking place within us. Likewise, when we read such seemingly mythical accounts of creation, we are likely to interpret them in terms of how the physical world was created. In a sense they are, but they are describing the physical world as it appears in consciousness.

> *All we are is that whole that manifests via 'functioning', whose functioning splits perceiving into supposed perceiver and supposed perceived, which are two divisions extended in time, the perceiving and the perceived divisions in consciousness, wherein all phenomenal manifestation seems to occur as long as the two divisions are held apparently apart by the time-notion in function.*
> —Wei Wu Wei

> *The mental and the material are two sides of one overall process that are (like form and content) separated only in thought and not in actuality. Rather, there is one energy that is the basis of all reality. There is never any real division between mental and material sides at any stage of the overall process.*
> —David Bohm

> *For his o'erarching and last lesson the greybeard sufi,*
> *In the fresh scent of the morning in the open air,*
> *On the slope of a teeming Persian rose-garden,*
> *Under an ancient chestnut-tree wide spreading its branches,*
> *Spoke to the young priests and students.*
> *Finally my children, to envelop each word, each part of the rest, Allah is all, all, all—immanent in every life and object, May-be at many and many-a-more removes—yet Allah, Allah, Allah is there.*
> *Has the estray wander'd far? Is the reason-why strangely hidden? Would you sound below the restless ocean of the entire world? Would you know the dissatisfaction? the urge and spur of every life; The something never still'd—never entirely gone? the invisible need of every seed? It is the central urge in every atom, (Often unconscious, often evil, downfallen,) To return to its Divine source and origin, however distant, Latent the same in subject and in object, without one exception.*
> —Walt Whitman

6 - The View of Quanta

And you are not engaged in any affair, nor do you recite concerning it any portion of the Quran, nor do you do any work but We are witnesses over you when you enter into it, and there does not lie concealed from your Lord the weight of an atom in the earth or in the heaven, nor anything less than that nor greater, but it is in a clear book.
—*Qur'an 10.61*

The discovery of the quantum of action shows us not only the natural limitation of classical physics, but, by throwing a new light upon the old philosophical problem of the objective existence of phenomena independently of our observations, confronts us with a situation hitherto unknown in natural science.
—*Niels Bohr*

Matter Myth

Quantum theory implied that to understand atomic particles one has to go beyond the old idea that matter is 'material stuff' that can be known through the senses, to descriptions of particles in terms of how they transform when subject to various interactions. It is how material objects respond when acted upon that tells us what they are.

Quantum theory describes the interaction of subatomic particles through the field concept. Particles and fields are complementary manifestations of the same thing. Gravitational and magnetic fields are invisible, but their effects can be determined.

The field concept was pioneered by Faraday, whose experiments on electric and magnetic fields established the idea. He viewed electrically charged particles as points at which the field became infinitely large. He argued that the field was the essential physical object and not the particle.

Maxwell developed the theory of electromagnetic fields and discovered that light is a wave of oscillating electric and magnetic fields propagating in space. Before, quantum theory, particles and fields were thought to be distinct entities. Particles were considered to be immutable and eternal. Fields emanated from particles and were responsible for the forces between them. Now a unified view is established: The dualism of energy and matter, particle and field were dissolved and everything could be seen to be interacting quantum fields. There isn't anything to material reality except the transformation and organization of field quanta.

Quantum theory states that the intensity of the field at a point in space is interpreted as the statistical probability for finding its associated quanta, the particles. What is meant by 'quantising a field' is analysing a field, such as electromagnetic wave in terms of its associated quanta, the photons. The intensity of the electromagnetic field at a point in space gives us the odds for finding a photon there.

The notion that reality is a set of fields that gives the probabilities for finding their associated quanta is the most important consequence of quantum field theory. Not only did the idea of matter disappear into the field concept, but the field specified the probability for finding quanta. The underlying reality is a set of fields representing each of the fundamental forces, but its manifestation is the particles.

Quantum theory represents a new phase in the understanding of the universe. The phase is actually the first to emerge after the birth of the cosmos from the womb of creation. The quantum worldview contrasts with the older Newtonian/Einsteinian classical world, in which its laws brought order to the visible world of earthly and celestial objects and events in time. The primary characteristic of the classical worldview is its determinism—a clockwork universe determined from the beginning to the end

6 - The View of Quanta

of time—and the assumption of objectivity, where things exist even if we do not directly observe them, independent of our consciousness.

In the quantum worldview, these commonsense classical assumptions of determinism and objectivity cannot be maintained. Although the quantum world is rationally comprehensible, it cannot be visualised in the classical world, mainly because the visual conventions we adopt from the world of ordinary objects do not apply to quantum 'objects'. We can speak of a stone or planet that can be both at rest and at a precise place and time. But it is meaningless to speak of a quantum particle such as an electron resting at a point in space and time. Electrons can materialise in places where classical physics says it is impossible.

Quantum theory is also non-deterministic, that is, the motion of electrons occurs at random and cannot be predicted. It is impossible to tell when an electron is going to move. We can only tell the probability of its location or motion. The most disturbing conflict with the classical worldview is the observer created reality. It was found that the theory requires that what an observer decides to measure, influences the measurement. The world isn't 'there' independent of our observing it. What is 'there' depends in part on what we choose to see. Reality is partially created by the observer. Einstein, until his death, rejected this seemingly mystical notion and maintained that nature was indifferent to human choices.

Quantum theory is mathematically consistent and agrees brilliantly with experiment. However, it remains disturbing to the mind that emerged into a rational worldview of determinism and objectivity. However, as already mentioned, the quantum reality was first to emerge from the womb of creation, therefore it precedes the classical reality of objects and events. Therefore it is synonymous with the pre-rational consciousness that has not differentiated into subject and object, space and time. The rational mind is yet to emerge, which corresponds with the emergence of the classical world of naïve realism.

The quantum world is fundamentally dualistic experientially. If you try to measure precisely both the position and its speed, you will find that it is not possible. Every time you measure its position, the speed changes, and vice versa. Most physicists do not think about the philosophical meaning of quantum theory. They simply apply the mathematics and discover the hidden laws. However, philosophers try to interpret the micro-world in terms of physical reality that is conceptually intelligible as well as mathematically consistent. As we have already seen, quantum theory began with Planck's quanta called h, which is a measure of the amount of discreteness in atomic processes, which implied that energy exchange happened in bursts.

> *Nothing is more important about quantum physics than this: it has destroyed the concept of the world as 'sitting out there'. The universe will never afterwards be the same.*
> —*John A. Wheeler*

CONFIRMATIONS

By the end of the nineteenth century, a few discoveries ushered in the new age of atomic physics.

In 1895, Wilhelm Roentgen discovered x-rays. Becquerel discovered radioactivity in 1896; in 1897, J. J. Thomson discovered the electron; and in 1898, the Curies isolated radium. The most puzzling was the emission of colored light from substances in certain conditions. Each chemical element has a definite and unique set of colored lines, called its spectrum. No one yet had any explanation for these phenomena.

Ernest Rutherford discovered that radioactive transformation of chemical elements, previously thought to be immutable, changed in the process of radioactivity. This discovery of the transmutation of the elements is the alchemist's objective. Rutherford was the first to gain insight into the structure of the atom. Following experimental evidence, he postulated the existence of the nucleus, the positively charged centre of the atom. The atom, previously thought to be without parts, is in fact the principle building block of the universe.

In 1911, Rutherford announced his model of the atom. Most

6 - The View of Quanta

of the mass of the atom was concentrated in a tiny, positively charged core, the nucleus, whereas the negatively charged electrons, with very small mass, formed a large cloud around the nucleus, held by electric forces, accounting for the size of the atom. The nucleus is 10,000 times smaller than the atom. According to classical physics, this model is unstable. The electron should radiate away its energy in the form of electromagnetic energy and collapse into the nucleus.

Niels Bohr worked briefly with Rutherford and took a quantum leap by applying the quantum principle. He assumed that the electrons in motion around the nucleus do not radiate continuous energy. He showed that Planck's idea of energy quantisation implied that only specific orbits for the electrons are allowed. The atom is stable because there is a minimum orbit such that the electron could not fall into the nucleus. When the electron drops from a high orbit to a lower one, it emits light in a quantised fashion. Because the energy of light is related to its colour, only specific colours can be emitted by atoms, thus explaining the spectra of light emitted by chemical elements. Bohr's model was the start of a new phase of thinking that broke off from the old classical paradigm. Atoms emitting light seemed to behave spontaneously and undeterministically. The conservation laws of classical physics seem to be violated, and thus a key symmetry in nature is broken. The revolutionary idea is that quantum particles do not move continuously in paths in space from one orbit to another. They jump, disappear completely and appear at a different orbit in an unpredictable manner.

Quantum theory implies that the vacuum of empty space actually consists of particles and anti-particles being spontaneously created and annihilated. Space looks empty only because the creation and destruction of all the quanta take place over very short times and distances. Everything that ever existed or can exist is already potentially there in the nothingness of space.

Heisenberg's uncertainty principle developed in 1927, states that the simultaneous determination of two paired quantities, for example, the position and momentum of a particle, has an unavoidable uncertainty. Together with Bohr, he formulated the

Copenhagen interpretation of quantum mechanics. The uncertainty principle also predicts that quanta can be created out of nothing for short time periods. The vacuum randomly fluctuates between being and nothingness. Because energy is uncertain for short periods of time, a quantum could come into existence in empty space and quickly disappear. Such a quantum is called a *virtual quantum*. It could become a real quantum if it had sufficient energy to do so. This process has been observed in experiments. A *vacuum fluctuation* consists of a particle and its anti-particle springing into virtual existence at a point in space and then immediately annihilating each other.

In 1926 Erwin Schrödinger developed the theory of wave mechanics. Wave mechanics was an independent formulation of quantum mechanics to Heisenberg's matrix mechanics. Wave mechanics mathematically described the behaviour of electrons and atoms. The central equation of wave mechanics, now known as the Schrödinger equation, turned out to be much simpler for physicists to solve in most cases. The Schrödinger equation plays the role of Newton's laws and conservation of energy in classical mechanics. It predicts the future behaviour of a dynamic system. It is a wave equation in terms of the wave function, which predicts analytically and precisely the probability of events or outcome. The detailed outcome is not strictly determined, but given a large number of events, the Schrödinger equation will predict the distribution of results.

Another important principle is the Pauli exclusion principle, formulated in 1925 by Wolfgang Pauli. This principle is significant because it explains why matter occupies space exclusively for itself and does not allow other material objects to pass through it, while at the same time allowing light and radiation to pass. It states that no two identical fermions may occupy the same quantum state simultaneously. The Pauli exclusion principle is one of the most important principles in physics, primarily because the three types of particles that make up ordinary matter: electrons, protons and neutrons—are all subject to it. Consequently, all material particles exhibit space-occupying nature. The Pauli exclusion principle underpins many of the characteristic properties of matter, from the large-scale stability of matter to the existence of the periodic table of the elements.

Most of the space between an atomic nucleus and an orbiting electron can be thought of as empty, and this is where the virtual effects has been found. This effect, called *vacuum polarisation* slightly changes the orbit of the electron. In accelerators, the collision of matter with antimatter provided the necessary energy to bring the virtual pair of particles fluctuating in the vacuum into real existence. Possibly the universe sprang into existence out of nothingness from a vacuum fluctuation resulting in the Big Bang. Stephen Hawking theorised the creation of elementary particles from black holes and argues that the universe exploded into being in a quantum-mechanical event.

> *In the case of electrons, the musical score is the wave function. As with the dancers, the electrons are thus participating in a common action based on a pool of information, rather than pulling or pushing on each other mechanically according to laws like those of classical physics.*
> —David Bohm

Implicate Wholeness

An alternative view was provided by the physicist David Bohm, who stated that the nature of things is not reducible to fragments or particles. He argues for a holistic view of the universe. He demands that we learn to regard matter and life as a whole, coherent domain, which he calls the implicate order. The objects in his universe, even the subatomic particles, are secondary; it is a process of movement, continuous unfolding and enfolding from a seamless whole that is fundamental.

Bohm describes his vision in this beautiful allegory:

> *Imagine an infinite sea of energy filling empty space, with waves moving around in there, occasionally coming together and producing an intense pulse. Let's say one particular pulse comes together and expands, creating our universe of space-*

time and matter. But there could well be other such pulses. To us, that pulse looks like a big bang; in a greater context, it's a little ripple. Everything emerges by unfoldment from the holomovement, then enfolds back into the implicate order. I call the enfolding process 'implicating', and the unfolding 'explicating'. The implicate and explicate together are a flowing, undivided wholeness. Every part of the universe is related to every other part but in different degrees.

Quantum 'stuff' consist of patterns of active relationships: electrons and photons, mesons and nucleons, which have a double life, as they are now particles, now waves, now mass, now energy, all in response to each other and to the environment. The wave/particle duality of quantum 'stuff' is the primal mind/body, subject/object relationship in the world and the core of all that, at higher levels, which we recognise as the mental and physical aspects of life.

> *The mental and the material are two sides of one overall process that are (like form and content) separated only in thought and not in actuality. Rather, there is one energy that is the basis of all reality. There is never any real division between mental and material sides at any stage of the overall process.*
> —David Bohm

In a quantum system of two or more particles, each particle has both 'thingy-ness' and 'relating-ness', the first due to its particle aspect and the second to its wave aspect. The wave aspect in a quantum system allows intimate relationships that don't exist in classical systems. Classical systems have external relationships only as a result of forces of attraction and repulsion which do not alter the inner qualities. But, in a group, electrons interfere with each other in that they overlap and merge and become part of a whole.

This is the most primal level of existence: a pattern of active relationships, the wave aspect of the wave/particle duality, that culminate in levels of consciousness as relationships at all levels/

6 - The View of Quanta

hierarchies of existence. When seeing consciousness as a quantum wave phenomena, mental life can be traced to its roots in the quantum field. The mind/body duality is a reflection of the wave/particle duality that underlies everything. Consciousness is a kind of quantum relationship of two or more particles with overlapping wave functions.

The background state of all consciousness on which all forms of thoughts and perceptions are written has the characteristic of unbroken wholeness. It occurs in materials that exist in state of 'condensed phases' and it refers to the amount of order existing in a system. Examples of this are magnets, superfluids, superconductors and lasers. They all have a degree of coherence in which the many atoms that make up the substance behave as one.

A special state condensed phase is the *Bose-Einstein condensate* where the many parts initially behave as a whole, but then become whole. The individual identities are lost entirely. It is only in such condensates, where individuality breaks down, that we can find quantum mechanical effects in large scale systems. In biological systems, condensed phases at normal temperatures exist in what is known as a pumped system. This is a system of vibrating electrically charged molecules in cell walls into which energy is pumped. The molecules emit photons at microwave frequencies. These molecules start to vibrate in unison after a certain energy threshold is reached. They do so increasingly until they form a Bose-Einstein condensate.

The Quran says that whatever is in the heavens and the earth glorifies Allah; meaning, is loyal to its prescribed path. Every created entity announces its nature and is true to it. Man is also true to His Creator in that he will never rest until he discovers His real Lord. By submitting to Him, he is freed. All pursuits, whether high or low, mental or physical, are steps towards that discovery. Man is programmed to seek contentment and peace, not realizing that his real nature is already that. He thinks that he can bring about contentment and peace by satisfying desires and strengthening attachments. What he is really attached to are the Lord's attributes—al-

Hayy, as-Samad, as-Salaam (The Everliving, the Everlasting, the Everpeaceful). Glorification implies devotion, connectedness, and therefore Tawhid/Unity. The electron has no choice but to be loyal to its path and the changes occur therein, according to the variations in circumstance. In that sense, we can say that it is totally devoted to, and therefore worships, its reality. In the same way, man is creature of devotion, adoration, loyalty, and therefore worship. He seeks and therefore he is sought. If he does not seek along the prescribed path of knowledge, he will be sought by afflictions, troubles, and tribulations which are all natural ways of reminding him to bring himself back to the path of Tawhid, through experience and knowledge.

—Shaykh Fadhlalla Haeri

Transcendence

When we recognise that, in the real world, light does not travel across space or time, a difficult conundrum in quantum physics becomes much easier to understand. In our image of reality, we observe energy travelling from one end of a light ray to the other. It is only natural to ask how the energy travels: Is it a wave? Or is it a particle? The answer, it appears, is both. In some situations light behaves as a continuous wave spreading out in space, but a wave without a medium. In other situations it behaves as a particle travelling through space, but a particle without mass. Physicists have accommodated these two strange and seemingly paradoxical conclusions by deciding that light is a 'wave-particle'. In certain circumstances it appears as a wave; in others as a particle.

But if we look at things from light's point of view, it is neither, because it did not travel through space and time and it needed no vehicle or mechanism of travel. It simply transcends both wave and particle. As far as light itself is concerned, there is no duality and no paradox. The physicist's paradox appears only when we mistake our image of reality with the 'thing in itself', and try to visualise light in concepts and terms appropriate to our image of

6 - The View of Quanta

reality—waves and particles.

The concept of 'matter', which is a leftover from the nineteenth century, still persists in our postmodern times in the cult of scientism. With relativity theory and quantum mechanics, and the new grand unifying theories of super-symmetry and super-strings, the whole notion of matter has become an absurdity.

In summary, quantum mechanics can be seen as an investigation of a level of cosmic reality that is inferred subjectively. It is the 'real' where conscious activities or patterns are functioning at the deepest level. In the waking consensual classic state there is a perception of a certain degree of rigidity, a fixed 'material' state. However, in deeper psychological states, such as dreaming, the rigidity is surrendered and all kinds of paradoxes manifest that appear to be illogical compared to the conventional waking state. These paradoxical quantum states exist at a depth of consciousness, a realm or a dimension of experience, that is inherently uncertain or indeterminate. It is a dimension within consciousness that is fluid in contrast with the rigid reality of classical physics.

And you see the mountains, thinking them rigid, while they will pass as the passing of clouds. The work of Allah, who perfected all things. Indeed, He is acquainted with that which you do.
—*Qur'an 27.88*

To see a world in a Grain of Sand,
And a Heaven in a Wild Flower,
Hold Infinity in the palm of your hand,
And eternity in an hour.
—*William Blake*

7 - The View of Mind

Surely We have created everything in measure.
—*Qur'an 54.59*

Magic of Mathematics

A fundamental question in science is: how is it that mathematics, which is a creation of the human mind without any empirical reference to external reality, should match reality so well? When we make the distinction between the reality we experience and the underlying reality, the correlation between mathematics and reality is not so surprising.

To answer such a question, it is useful to begin by understanding the difference between Western and Eastern notions of measure. Now, in the West, the notion of measure has, from very early times, played a key role in determining the general self-worldview and the way of life implicit in such a view. Thus among the Ancient Greeks, from whom we derive a large part of our fundamental notions, keeping everything in its right measure was regarded as one of the essentials of a good life.

In this regard, measure was not looked on in its modern sense as being primarily some sort of comparison of an object with an external standard or unit. Rather, this latter procedure was regarded as a kind of outward display or appearance of a deeper 'inner measure', which played an essential role in everything. When something went beyond its proper measure, this meant not merely that it was not conforming to some external standard of what was right but, much more, that it was inwardly out of harmony, so that it was bound to lose its integrity and break up into fragments.

One can obtain some insight into this way of thinking by considering the earlier meanings of certain words. The Latin word *mederi* meaning 'to heal' (the root of the modern term *medicine*) is based on a Proto-Indo-European root meaning 'to measure'. This reflects the view that physical health is to be regarded as the outcome of a state of right inward measure in all parts and processes of the body.

Similarly, the word *moderation*, which describes one of the prime ancient notions of virtue, is based on the same root, and this shows that such virtue was regarded as the outcome of a right inner measure underlying man's social actions and behavior. Again, the word *meditation*, which is based on the same root, implies a kind of weighing, pondering, or measuring of the whole process of thought, which could bring the inner activities of the mind to a state of harmonious measure. So, physically, socially and mentally, awareness of the inner measure of things was seen as the essential key to a healthy, happy, harmonious life.

It is clear that measure is to be expressed in more detail through proportion or ratio. *Ratio* is the Latin word from which our modern *reason* is derived. In the ancient view, reason is seen as insight into a totality of ratio or proportion, regarded as relevant inwardly to the very nature of things (and not only outwardly as a form of comparison with a standard or unit).

Of course, this ratio is not necessarily merely a numerical proportion. Rather, it is in general a qualitative sort of universal proportion or relationship. The essential reason or ratio of a thing, then, is the totality of inner proportions in its structure, and in the process in which it forms, maintains itself, and ultimately dissolves. In this view, to understand such ratio is to understand the 'innermost being' of that thing.

In the East, the notion of measure only gave allusions toward the immeasurable, which is regarded as the primary reality. Thus, in Sanskrit there is the word *matra*, which means 'measure' in the musical sense and is evidently close to the Greek word *metron*. But then there is another word, *maya*, obtained from the same

7 - The View of Mind

root, which means 'illusion'. In this view the entire structure and order of forms, proportions and 'ratios' that present themselves to ordinary perception and reason are regarded as a veil, covering the true reality, which cannot be perceived by the senses and of which nothing can be said or thought.

What we can do is give full attention and creative energies to bring clarity and order into the totality of the field of measure. This involves not only the outward display of measure in terms of external units but also inward measure, such as health of the body, moderation in action, and meditation, which gives insight into the measure of thought. The latter is particularly important because, as has been seen, the illusion that the self and the world are broken into fragments originates in the kind of thought that goes beyond its proper measure, and confuses its own product with the same independent reality. To end this illusion requires insight, not only into the world as a whole, but also into how the instrument of thought is working. Such insight implies an original and creative act of perception into all aspects of life, mental and physical, both through the senses and through the mind.

> *If mathematics was traditionally considered an intellectual science of sorts, this is because its principles can be discovered within oneself without the need for transmission. The special sense of certainty that comes from mathematical knowledge was seen as deriving from the fact that mathematics is an expression of the unitary, intelligible order that underlies apparent reality and forms the bedrock of the soul. Unlike transmitted knowledge, mathematical truths, once understood, are seen to be necessarily so, because they conform with the reality that shapes cosmos and soul. Nonetheless, to the degree that mathematics operates on the basis of data coming from outside the self, it was not considered a pure intellectual science. It partakes of a lesser degree of certainty and was commonly considered 'intermediate' (mutawassit) between transmitted and intellectual.*
>
> —William Chittick

The science of mathematics is purely a creation of the mind. Mathematics is that body of knowledge that is arrived at by pure reason, and does not rely upon any observations of the phenomenal world. It is free from the limitations imposed by the particular way human minds create their experience of the underlying. As such it is probably the closest the human mind can come to understanding the thing-in-itself.

The only thing that pure mathematics depends upon is the notion of distinction. I experience things as they are distinct or differentiated from each other. I can distinguish between the black ink and the white paper of this page. Even in the underlying reality there is distinction. We may not know what the thing-in-itself is really like, but we can measure its separation in the space-time interval from another thing-in-itself. If there was no distinction in the cosmos, there would be no difference of any kind, no experience whatsoever. The existence of distinction is as undeniable as the existence of experience itself.

If there are distinctions, we can count them. Counting is the beginning of measurement. From counting comes the concept of number. We can add numbers together, leading to multiplication of numbers, and their opposites: subtraction and division. From this simple arithmetic comes the concept of nothing: zero; and beyond zero, the negative. Numbers are not part of our direct experience, but it is a concept we accept. By counting all the numbers we arrive at the notion of infinity.

And between the rational numbers we discover an infinity of irrational or transcendental numbers that cannot be expressed as the ratio of two integers, for example, numbers such as 'pi', the ratio of the circumference of a circle to its diameter, or 'e', the base of natural logarithms. They can be defined, but never written down exactly as a number, for they go on forever, to an infinite number of decimal places. All this from the notion of distinction.

And there is more: Any positive number has a square root, the number that when multiplied by itself produces that number. The square root of 1 is 1; of 4 is 2; and of 8 is 2.828... (another irrational number that goes on forever). But what, asked math-

7 - The View of Mind

ematicians of negative numbers, multiplied by itself gives -1? Nothing in the range has so far been discovered. Any number, positive or negative, when multiplied by itself results in a positive number. So mathematicians defined the square root of -1 to be a totally new number, an 'imaginary' number, not part of the range of 'real' numbers, and gave it the symbol 'i'. From this arose a new and even larger set of numbers, the so-called 'complex' numbers that are a combination of real and imaginary numbers. And these, it turned out, were invaluable in helping mathematicians solve equations that had no solution in the realm of real numbers. Moreover, the solutions applied to the real world.

Out of this panoply of numbers, a most remarkable and intriguing relationship appeared. The irrational number 'pi', the irrational number 'e', and the imaginary number 'i', come together in one of simplest and most beautiful equations ever: 'e to the power of i times pi = -1', known as Euler's identity. Many mathematicians have eulogised over the significance and beauty of this equation. Out on the very edge of the number theory, a relationship is discovered that seems to show it is all in some way pre-ordained. Little wonder that some mathematicians feel that God is to be found in the beauty and perfection of mathematics.

That these three seemingly unconnected numbers should be related in such a simple way was startling enough, but even more was in store. This simple equation is the basic equation of any wave motion. Every wave—from a wave on water, the air waves coming from a violin string, to light waves—can be expressed as a combination of simple equations of this form. It also expresses the orbits of the planets, the swing of a pendulum and the oscillation of an atom. In fact, every single motion in the cosmos can ultimately be reduced to an equation of this form. The whole of quantum physics depends upon it. If mathematicians had not discovered this most remarkable relationship, then the strange story of the quantum could never have been told. It is no wonder then, that in the end, all science comes down to mathematics. The very fact that it is not based upon phenomena is why it is probably the best approximation to the underlying reality that we have.

The concepts of both zero and infinity arose as a result of higher abstraction of consciousness: to try to reach beyond the known. Infinity is not a number. Infinity is not a quantity or a location in space-time, nor is it a process in a cause-and-effect event. Infinity cannot be attained by the addition or subtraction of any number, and it is not possible to move closer to or away from infinity. Therefore infinity is unattainable and unquantifiable. The same goes for zero. They are both indivisible, irreducible and beyond quantification. They are both a representation of the timeless self-state, of emptiness and wholeness.

To invent the concept of numbers, humans started with the idea of a localised point of view of the separate self, and of the other, and of differences representing objective quantities. The concept of the number 1 is the source of all quantified numbers and all differences. It is the numerical idea representation of the self-identity. All worldly transactions are quantifiable, numerically based motions or stages or processes that are valid only from a separate self of a subjective/objective point of view. Both zero and infinity are intrinsically numberless states that exist prior to, and beyond, quantity.

If the doors of perception were cleansed, everything would appear to man as it is, infinite.
—William Blake

Incompleteness

By the end of the nineteenth century, David Hilbert was one of the most important mathematicians of the time, having made fundamental contributions to practically all of the main areas of pure mathematics as well as applications of mathematics to physics. Off and on from the end of the nineteenth century through the first third of the twentieth century, he was also very much concerned with the foundations of mathematics and was troubled by contradictions found by Georg Cantor and Bertrand Russell in the theory of sets which was the most general mathematical theory to have been developed for foundational purposes.

7 - The View of Mind

Hilbert's idea was to secure the foundations of mathematics on a solid basis, and to do this in a convincing way, he proposed to model mathematical reasoning in formal systems so as to be able to establish precise results about them. Hilbert's first aim was to show for stronger and stronger systems for mathematics, beginning with arithmetic, so that they are consistent.

Because the concept of a formal system is explained in precise mathematical terms, the question of its consistency is a precise mathematical problem. Hilbert wanted to apply mathematics to secure mathematics, but he conceived of the enterprise as a new subject that he called meta-mathematics.

In 1931 Kurt Gödel, with his incompleteness theorems, proved that Hilbert's program was unattainable. His two theorems state inherent limitations of all but the most trivial systems of arithmetic in mathematics. The theorems state that any effectively generated theory capable of expressing elementary arithmetic cannot be both consistent and complete. He showed that the internal consistency of the axiomatic method is limited. *Axiomatic* means self-evident absolute truths. Such a system will always be inherently incomplete. He was able to demonstrate that true statements exist that cannot be proved, meaning that mathematics is incomplete and inconsistent. It is incomplete because there will always exist mathematical truths that cannot be demonstrated. The system is also inconsistent because it is possible for a statement and its negation to exist simultaneously within the same system.

Gödel's Theorem has many profound implications, both for science and for philosophy. Gödel's message is that we will never know the final secret of the universe by dualistic, rational discursive thought alone. It is impossible for human beings to ever formulate a complete description of the natural numbers. There will always be arithmetic truths that escape our ability to fence them in by any kind of finite analysis. We can spend infinite amounts of time conducting endless investigations. But we will never achieve ultimate success. There is no final verdict in the court of science leading to absolute truth.

Like Heisenberg's uncertainty principle, this notion has captured the public imagination with the idea that there are absolute limits to what can be known. More specifically, it is said that Gödel's Theorem tells us that there are mathematical truths that can never be proved. Among postmodernists, it is used to support scepticism about objective truth. Nothing can be known for sure.

One of the most prominent proponents of the claim that Gödel's Theorem proves that mind is not mechanical is Roger Penrose, who said that there must be more to human thinking than can ever be achieved by a computer. However, he thinks that there must be a scientific explanation of how the mind works, albeit in its non-mechanical way, and that ultimately must be given in physical terms, but that current physics is inadequate to do the job.

Stephen Hawking and Freeman Dyson, among others, have come to the conclusion that Gödel's Theorem implies that there cannot be a Theory of Everything. The supposed consequences of the incompleteness theorem for both the nature of mind and the laws of the universe are quite interesting and should be examined on their own merits.

Gödel's Theorem demonstrates the principle of the inexhaustibility of pure mathematics in the sense of the never-ending need for new axioms. There can never be any absolutes regarding mentally generated ideas.

Metaphysical Symbolism

Mathematical symbols are not just a result of any individual's thoughts or ideas but represent a metaphysical reality of things that exist in the universe. For example, a circle is seen manifested. We do not see the centre of it, but the circle cannot be constructed without the centre point, which serves as a symbol for unity, source, and the controlling point. So the centre here becomes a metaphysical entity whose presence we may not feel but is required for the circle to be manifested.

Accordingly, the Islamic *La ilaha illa Allah* means no divinity without the soul divinity, no god but God, no part without

7 - The View of Mind

whole, no reflection without the Source.

The spiritual equivalent is that it is through symbols that one is awakened. It is through symbols that one is transformed, and it is through symbols that one expresses. It is through geometry that the personality and character of numbers are revealed, providing still another means of getting to know the cosmic process of nature.

The creation of shapes through the use of numbers and geometry, as mathematical expressions, recalls the archetypes reflected through the world of symbols. Mathematics, then, is a language of the intellect, a means of spiritual hermeneutics whereby one can move from the sensible to the intelligible world. Geometric patterns were developed in order to provide the viewer with objects of contemplation that would trigger an innate aesthetic reaction, and thus a religious experience of the heavens. It was believed that this triggering was possible because the patterns were well proportioned and harmonious and because their geometric basis instantiated heavenly prototypes. This is the sacred approach to design that made abstract transcendent beauty accessible.

Since ancient times, there has been interest in things that are considered to incorporate within their intrinsic relationships, both mathematical and geometrical, a universal truth. Resonances were seen to be present from the smallest to largest elements of the natural world and, in this, a unity was perceived. It was believed that these geometries were derived from, or described, the basic laws of the nature.

Geometry in Islam is the outcome of studying or contemplating the natural forms and cosmology. This way of looking at it consists in abstracting its qualities through scientific laws and regulations, its underlying mathematics and its inherent principle of structure. Wisdom traditions observed all of creation as an emanation from the One, and proceed on the revelation that He shares with nature a commonality of structure and proportion that is quantifiable through mathematics.

Conversely, all of the creations of man and nature are viewed as forms observable through mathematical laws of similitude, symmetry and geometry. The beauty sensed by man in a snow crystal or a flower depends as much on its level of maturation during its life cycle of growth patterns as it does on its geometrical order, to reflect a higher and more profound order. It follows that all shapes, surfaces and lines are arranged in conformity with the proportioning system of beauty, and, in this, a unity was perceived that is believed to be the sacred. Equilibrium is a characteristic spiritual quality in Islam. Islam is, in cyclic terms, a return to a primal equilibrium, and its geometrical crystallisation is a result of this equilibrium.

Sacred Projections

The sacred is the projection of the celestial Centre into the cosmic periphery, or of the 'Motionless Mover' into the flux of things. To feel this concretely is to possess the sense of the sacred, and thereby the instinct of adoration, devotion and submission. The sense of the sacred is the awareness—in the world of that which may or may not be—of that which cannot not be, and whose immense remoteness and miraculous proximity we experience at one and the same time.

Mathematics is the underlying order of all natural phenomena. Artists understood nature deeply through the mathematical relations among substances, such as the growth pattern of plants, the distribution or arrangement of leaves on a stem and the arrangements of petals in flower. After studying and understanding it, a theoretical system of proportion was developed that helped them to create various varieties of patterns.

All of the laws and systems with which the universe works can be symbolically represented in a geometrical diagram. The natural divisions of the year, and the rhythms of Sun, Moon and Earth that define it, are a fundamental key to cosmological numbers. The circle surpasses all other geometric patterns as the symbol of cosmic unity, its inner core or hidden centre becoming the timeless moment of the revolutions of time and the dimensionless point of the encompassing space. The indications of periods of time and directions in space occur in pattern form as intervals around the perimeter of this primal circle.

This projection of three-dimensional space from a two-dimensional pattern illustrates the Islamic philosophical doctrine of emanation, in which manifestation is asserted through the dimension. 'Our' world is at the gross end of the emanation and exists in three-dimensional coordinates. The two-dimensional plane is used as a convention to symbolise the more subtle levels of emanation and indicate the direction of the source of manifestation.

Freedom is not a reaction; freedom is not choice. It is man's pretence that because he has choice he is free. Freedom is pure observation without direction, without fear of punishment and reward. Freedom is without motive; freedom is not at the end of the evolution of man but lies in the first step of his existence. In observation one begins to discover the lack of freedom. Freedom is found in the choiceless awareness of our daily existence and activity.
—JidduKrishnamurti

8 - The View of the Biosphere

We created the human being of an extraction of clay, then We set him, a drop, in a receptacle secure, then We created of the drop a clot then We created of the clot a tissue then We created of the tissue bones then We garmented the bones in flesh; thereafter We produced him as another creature. So blessed be God, the fairest of creators.
—*Qur'an 23.12*

Bio Emergence

The first simple organisms—bacteria and algae—having no senses, were aware in only the most rudimentary way: no form, no structure, just the vaguest glimmer of awareness. Their picture of the world is nothing but an extremely dim smudge of colour, virtually nothing compared to the richness and detail of human experience.

When multicellular organisms evolved, so did this sensing capacity. Cells emerged that specialised in sensing light, vibration, pressure, or changes in chemistry. These cells formed sensory organs, and as they developed, their ability to absorb information increased. Eyes are not only sensitive to light. They react differently to different frequencies, and can tell from which direction the light is coming. The faintest smudge of the bacterium's experience had begun to take on different hues and shapes. Forms had begun to emerge on the canvas of consciousness.

With the emergence of nervous systems, processing sense

data and distributing it to other parts of the organism became possible. Before long, the flow of information required a central processing system, and with it a more integrated picture of the world appeared. As brains evolved, new features were added to consciousness. With reptiles, the limbic system appeared, an area of the brain associated with emotion. Feeling had been added.

In birds and mammals the nervous system grew yet more complex, developing a cortex around it. With the cortex came other new abilities. A dog chasing a cat around a corner holds some image in its mind of the cat it can no longer see. Creatures with a cortex have memory and recognition. They can pay attention and show intention.

With primates, the cortex grew into the larger, more complex neocortex, adding yet more features to consciousness. The most significant of these was the ability to use symbols. Not only did this ability enable simple reasoning, it also led to a new form of communication: symbolic language.

This new ability of speech/language has expanded our consciousness in several ways. Our experience of space expanded as we learnt of events beyond our immediate sensory environment. And as we learnt of events that had happened before our own lives, our experience of time expanded. As well as using speech to communicate with each other, we can also use it to communicate with ourselves, inside our own minds. We can think to ourselves in words. Of all the developments that came from language, this has probably been the most significant.

THINKING MACHINE

Thinking allows us to conjure up associations to past experiences. In a similar way, thinking expanded our appreciation of the future. Thinking in words opened our minds to reason. We could ask questions: Why do stars move? How do our bodies function? What is matter? A whole new dimension had been added to our consciousness: understanding. We could form hypotheses and beliefs about the world in which we found ourselves.

We could also begin to understand ourselves. We could

8 - The View of the Biosphere

think about our own conscious experiences. We became aware not only of the many aspects and qualities of our consciousness, but also of the faculty of consciousness itself. We are aware of the fact that we are conscious. Consciousness could now reflect not only upon the nature of the world it experienced, but also on the nature of consciousness itself. Self-reflective consciousness had emerged.

The brain is part of nature, but the mind is not part of the brain. The mind, or consciousness, is the interior dimension, the exterior correlate of which is the objective brain. The mind is an 'I,' the brain is an 'It'. The brain, like anything else empirical in nature, can be known by empirical analytical investigation, but the mind can only be known by introspection, communication and interpretation. You can look at a brain, but you must talk to a mind, and that requires not just observation but interpretation.

Our normal waking consciousness is at its root unstable, ever moving, jumping from one perception to another, one feeling to another, and one thought to another. We can never hold it still or focus it at a point for long. Like the quantum nature of matter, the more we try to hold our consciousness to a fixed point, the greater the uncertainty in its energy will become. So when we focus and narrow our consciousness to a fixed centre, it is all the more likely to suddenly jump with a great rush of energy to some seemingly unrelated aspect of our inner life. We all have such experiences each moment of the day. As in our daily work, we try to focus our mind upon some problem only to suddenly experience a shift to some other domain in ourselves; another image or emotional current intrudes then vanishes again, like an ephemeral virtual particle in quantum theory.

A number of scientists, among them quantum physicists Amit Goswami and Fred Alan Wolf, attempted to construct a model of the brain and consciousness based on quantum mechanics. Here the quantum equation of the self-referential system of the brain/mind must continually be modified by the repeated measurement of interactions. As a result of the feedback, the quantum possibility waves of a self-referential system gradually become conditioned. The probability of actualising formerly experienced states gradually gains greater weight.

The inner sea of quantum effects in the brain is in some way coupled to our ever-flowing consciousness. When our consciousness focuses on a point, and we concentrate on some abstract problem or outer phenomenon, the physical events in the brain, the pattern of impulses, shifts in some ordered way. In a sense, the probability waves of a number of quantum systems in different parts of the brain are brought into resonance, and our consciousness is able momentarily to create an ordered pattern that manifests physically through the brain. The thought, feeling, or perception is momentarily grounded in physical reality, brought from the realm of the spiritually potential into outer actuality. This focused ordering of the probability waves of many quantum systems requires an enormous amount of energy, but this can be borrowed in the quantum sense for a short instance of time.

Thus we have through this quantum borrowing, a virtual quantum state that is the physical embodiment of a thought, feeling, perception, and so forth. However, as this can only be held for a short time, the quantum debt must be paid and the point of our consciousness is forced to jump to some other quantum state, perhaps in another region of the brain. Thus our thoughts are jumbled up with emotions, perceptions, fantasy images.

Based on the quantum model, experience consists of a perceived split of the world into one part (the subject, which may sometimes be implicit) that experiences the other part (object) as separate from it. How does the one world of matter separate into two, subject and object? The implicit or explicit subject of our local experiences is a local, personal 'I' that we call the self. But the implicit subject of the non-local experience is neither local nor personal. It is non-local and transpersonal.

Out of the self-referential measurement itself simultaneously arises a subject, the quantum self that measures, that chooses, that observes, and the objects that are observed. The subject-object dualism appears due to the act of a localized observing or measuring where there is only one system without division, therefore creating the illusion of a separate self.

In this description, dualism is avoided because ultimately

there is Oneness in which division is only an appearance, allowing subjects and objects to be treated on the same footing. Objects, such as the material body, have upward causation, affecting the mind by virtue of the laws of quantum possibility dynamics that they follow. The subject, which is the mind, has downward causation that comes from its freedom of selectivity to construct actuality from possibility, creating manifestation. These properties of consciousness, transcendence, unity, and self-reference, derived from the requirement that consciousness collapse the quantum wave function without raising any new paradox, are also the characteristics of consciousness that Gnostics from every age have declared, based on their direct realisation.

This self-reference is also the most important brain-mind paradox: How is it that we can refer to ourselves? The two paradoxes, self-reference and quantum measurement, find simultaneous resolution if we posit additionally that the brain has quantum machinery in addition to the neuronal machinery that act together as amplifying measurement apparatuses for the quantum.

The Making of Memory

A well-known characteristic of learning is that learning an activity reinforces the probability of the same subsequent activity. This is the effect we see here. In essence, learning increases the likelihood that, after the completion of measurement, the quantum-mechanical states of the tangled-hierarchical quantum-system/measurement-apparatus will correspond to a prior learned state. In other words, learning biases the quantum dynamics of the brain-mind and thus reduces the access to its full potentiality. Before learning, the possibility pool from which consciousness chooses its states spans the mental states common to all people in all places at all times. With learning, certain responses gradually gain greater weight over others, responses that we call personal.

Fairly early in physical development, learning accumulates and conditioned response patterns begin to dominate the brain-mind's behaviour, despite the fact that the versatility of the quantum system is always available for new creative experiences of 'primary awareness', which involves the quantum-self modality. When the creative potency of the quantum system is not engaged, when the primary awareness events are not attended, the 'secondary-awareness' processes of memory-replay dominate. The tangled hierarchy of the systems of the brain-mind, in effect, becomes a simple hierarchy of the learned programs, the representations of past experiences. At this stage, the creative uncertainty as to 'who the chooser is' of a conscious experience involving the quantum self diminishes. Then we begin to identify with a separate, individual self, the ego, which perceives apparent continuity in the form of a stream of consciousness that it thinks it chooses on the basis of its past experiences, that presumably has 'free will.' But in truth, this so-called free will of the ego-identity exists only to the extent that the conditioning is completely deconstructed by the death of the apparent individual self.

Underlying all time, space, energy and matter is the primordial consciousness, undifferentiated and whole, complete within itself, creating, sustaining and destroying all form and substance appearing to arise. The underlying state, the latent potential from which all thoughts, forms and expressions arise, is consciousness itself. This potentiality, when reflected upon, creates apparent differentiations that we observe as life.

From the smallest microcosm of energy particles to the greatest macrocosm of the universe, the underlying essence providing for all expressions is consciousness. Consciousness is the principle organising the systems creating form and substance through the inherent self-reflective quality of its nature.

From within the emptiness of the void, the creative potential gave light to infinite possibilities. The potential for life arose within itself, just as we experience each moment of the day and how to live it. This self-reflective quality of the universe is like a wave moving across an infinite ocean of possibilities. The ripples of consciousness create a dynamic that manifests as opposites: expansive/contractive, positive/negative, yang/yin, light/dark. These points of contrast manifest as the light and darkness. Galaxies bring forth the light through the polarisation of con-

8 - The View of the Biosphere

sciousness. The fields created through this polarisation create the whirling vortices that spur the creation of star systems, which manifest the consciousness through form and substance.

> *Evolution may be the result of an interplay between habits and creativity. New forms and patterns of organisation appear spontaneously, and are subject to natural selection. Those that survive are more likely to appear again as new habits build up, and through repetition they become increasingly habitual.*
> —Rupert Sheldrake

SELF-ORGANIZATION

All life systems involve the interface of opposites relating to each other forming patterns: expansion and contraction, centrifugal and centripetal, outer and inner, light and dark, proton and electron, positive and negative, yang and yin. The relationships between opposites define the system. The system has an attractive force, the receptive, yin, negative energy, and a repulsive force, the projective, yang, or positive energy pattern. Within each atom lies both the attractive and repulsive forces, and through the interaction with other atoms in its environment it is either attracted or repulsed by the other systems of organising intelligence in its environment.

The interaction between the positive and negative energy particles within the atom defines the boundaries of the atom and gives it its attractive and repulsive characteristics. This interaction creates a magnetic field. An energetic connection is made between the attractive and repulsive forces, and this relationship helps preserve the characteristics of that individual atom.

These patterns are called elements and compounds. Atoms organising by their attractive negative yin energies and repulsive positive yang energies create chains of atoms that are called molecules. Molecules are systems of atoms operating together in a way that perpetuates the patterns in which the organising intelligence is expressing the consciousness within itself. The more complex the energy pattern, the more evolved the life form.

At one end of the molecule there is a positive charge and on the other, a negative charge. A life-force current runs through the molecule and a field is created around it. Interaction with attractive and repulsive forces and positive and negative fields in its environment causes the molecule to adapt to patterns that support its existence. All life forms are attracted to forces that support their existence and are repulsed by those that do not.

The more articulated and evolved the molecular structure, the more intelligence develops. Thus intelligence is the systemisation of consciousness into complex patterns of expression. Through the innate drive for consciousness to be expressed, molecular structures evolve into increasingly more complex systems that express more intelligent life forms. The whole process of life is evolving consciousness to its highest expression. Life is a mechanism for growing consciousness.

Molecular structures form the building blocks for cells. Cells are simple life forms expressing consciously within a greater system of organising intelligence, such as a tissue or an organ. As a cell divides, the chromosomes within it align by their polar field. There is a current that flows through the cell, extending the life force throughout the cell. The positive charge is reflected on the top and the negative on the bottom, and a magnetic field lies around the cell, which gives it attractive and repulsive forces.

Within the body lies the collective strength of all the cells. The entire body is electrically charged, and a polar field lies around the body, an electromagnetic field that is popularly known as the aura. On top of the head lies the positive pole and at the base of the spine lies the negative pole. The life force runs up through the centre of the spine through the nerve core. The nerves branch out from the spine into all of the extremities, drawing the life-force energy throughout the body. The underlying innate intelligence is conducted through this life-force energy.

Emergence

When we look at the world, we do not see consciousness 'out there'. All we see are the various forms and qualities that consciousness has taken on. To us the 'material world' appears to be devoid of consciousness.

The reason we do not find consciousness in the world we observe is because consciousness is not part of the picture generated in our minds. It is the fabric on which the picture is painted. But when we mistakenly assume that the picture of reality painted in our minds is the underlying reality, we find ourselves presented with a very difficult question regarding consciousness: How does conscious experience arise or emerge from matter? This is the so-called 'hard question' to which many scientists and philosophers are currently devoting considerable time and attention.

The question these people are actually asking has more to do with our image of reality than the fundamental reality. They are asking how it is that a complex network of neurons can give rise to a conscious experience. How does something as immaterial as consciousness arise from something as unconscious as the material world? Is it a result of the complex patterning of data across the neural net? Is it due to quantum coherence effects in microtubules within the neurons? Or is it something else?

What all these approaches have in common is that they are trying to explain consciousness in terms of phenomena that belong to our image or model of reality, which is itself a manifestation within consciousness.

The so-called 'hard question' is actually a mistaken question. When we distinguish between the two realities, the question disappears, to be replaced by its opposite: How is it that matter, space, time, colour, sound, form, and all the other qualities we experience emerge in consciousness? What is the process of manifestation within the mind?

> *No problem can be solved from the same consciousness that created it.*
> —*Albert Einstein*

Dreamscapes

In our dreams we are aware of sights, sounds and sensations

happening around us. We see dream colours, hear dream music, smell dream fragrances, and taste dream food. We are aware of our bodies; we think and reason; we feel fear, anger, and love. We experience other people as individuals separate from us, speaking and interacting with us. In the dream it all seems very real and appears to be happening 'out there' in the world around us. But when we awaken, we realise that everything in the dream, including our own body, was a creation in the mind. It was 'all just a dream'.

It was just a dream insofar as the image created in the mind was not based on physical reality. It was created from memories, hopes, fears, unconscious needs and other influences. There is no input from the outside world.

The difference with waking consciousness is that the image created in the mind is based primarily on sensory data drawn from our physical surroundings. This gives our waking experience a consistency not found in dreams. We do not suddenly find ourselves transported to a completely different location, conversing with someone we have never met before. We do not find physical reality transforming before our very eyes. When we are awake, the images created in the mind bear a direct relationship to the physical world around us.

Our sleeping dreams are private affairs. Whatever I may be dreaming usually has little similarity to what another person may be dreaming. They are based on different inputs. Our waking experiences, on the other hand, are based on very similar sets of data. The light reflected from a tree to my eye is the same as that reflected to another person. The images created in our minds are, as far as we can tell, identical. We are likely to find ourselves agreeing on everything, right down to the finest details of the colour and structure of a leaf or thorn. It is a consensual. This confirms our assumption that we are experiencing reality as it is 'out there', around us.

It is hard to come to terms with the fact that our normal waking experience of reality is a manifestation within our consciousness, but in many other instances we readily accept that we create our experiences. A classic example of reality creation

8 - The View of the Biosphere

that has long fascinated medical researchers is the phantom limb phenomenon. A person who has lost an arm or leg may continue to have sensations that seem to come from the missing limb. For some reason the nerve fibres that once reached down into the leg or arm, although no longer connected to any sensory receptors, are still sending signals to the brain. The brain gives the sense as if the limb is still there and creates the corresponding experience. This can be most disconcerting for the person concerned, who may feel an irresistible urge to scratch an itch in an arm or leg that is not there.

The opposite phenomenon can occur in situations in which the body has become unusually still. Arms and legs that are definitely there in the physical world can completely disappear from experience. Normally, we know where our arms and legs are, even when not looking at them or touching them, because any bodily movement, however slight, triggers impulses in the body's sense receptors located in joints, muscles, the skin and other organs that inform the brain of changes in position, tension, and such in the internal organs.

When the body becomes very still, as can happen in states of deep meditation, these receptors may no longer be triggered and the flow of data from them can die away. The brain no longer has the necessary information from which to construct its image of the body, and so the arm or leg ceases to exist in awareness. Conversely, it only takes a minute movement, a flexing of one's little toe, say to trigger the flow of data, and the missing arm or leg immediately returns to awareness.

We dismiss many other creations of the mind as hallucinations. These are typically experiences that occur under the influence of drugs, and during illness, extreme fatigue, or stress. For one reason or another, the electrochemical processes are modified in some way, leading the brain to generate a different image of reality. One may perceive unusual colors or patterns, perceive time and space differently, or experience some other 'non-ordinary' manifestation in consciousness.

We call such images 'hallucinations' because they do not concur with our normal experience of reality, or with the reality that other people experience. We say we are seeing things that are not really there. But, surprising as it may seem at first, this is what we are doing all the time. Even in normal, everyday perception, the kind we all agree upon, we are seeing things that are not really there. Color, sound, smell, and all the other qualities of experience are not qualities of the physical world.

The fact that we create our experience of reality does not imply that there is no underlying reality. There is something that gives rise to my perception, and to your perception and to the perception of a bird sitting on a branch. But we know nothing of that event directly. All we know are the experiences created in our minds.

Culturescapes

The set of sensory organs with which we have been endowed only offers us a small window on reality. Much of the information in the physical reality is filtered out, leaving us with a very partial set of data with which to construct our picture of the world. In this respect, the thing-in-itself is far more than our experience ever reveals to us. It contains a multitude of features of which we have no awareness whatsoever, and in many instances no concept of either.

We like to believe that our perceptions are of the real world, the physical world. But the world we spend most of our time perceiving is not just any segment of the physical world, but a highly socialised part of the physical world that has been built into cities, political organisations and technologies. So our perception may indeed be realistic, but it is so only with respect to a very tailored segment of reality, a consensus reality, a small selection of things we have agreed are 'real' and 'important'.

Thus, within our particular cultural framework, we can easily set up what seem to be excellent scientific experiments that will show that our perceptions are indeed realistic, in the sense that we agree with each other on these selected items from our consensus reality.

A culture is as a group of people who, through various historical processes, have come to an agreement that certain human potentials they know of are *good, holy, natural.* They are defined as the essence of being human. Other potentials, also known to the culture, are considered *bad, evil,* or *unnatural.* The culture actively inhibits the development of these potentials in its children, not always successfully. Large number of other human potentials are simply not known to that particular culture, and although some of them develop owing to accidental circumstances in a particular person's life, most do not develop for lack of stimulation. Some of these potentials remain latent, capable of being developed if circumstances are right in later life. Others disappear completely through not being developed at an early, critical stage.

Each of us is simultaneously the beneficiary of his or her cultural heritage and the victim and slave of his or her culture's narrowness. Like almost all people in all cultures at all times, we think our local culture is best and other people are inferior, uncivilised, or savages.

By the time an ordinary person reaches childhood, he or she has attained a basic membership in the consensus reality of his culture. A normal child has a pretty good idea of the dos and don'ts of the culture, and behaves in generally acceptable fashion. Many of the potentials present at the time of his or her birth are gone by now, but consensus reality has been formed from the few that have been cultivated. One of the main ways in which consciousness is shaped to fit consensus reality is through the medium of language. The word for an object focuses a child's perception onto a specific thing considered important by the culture. Social approval for this kind of behaviour gives words great power. As a child gradually grows in mastery of language, the language structure and its effect on consciousness grow at an exponential rate. The tyranny of words is one of the most difficult things from which we must try to free ourselves.

Because of the power over physical reality given to them by their consensus reality, adults are the most free, yet, because they are the most thoroughly indoctrinated in consensus reality, they are the most bound. They receive many rewards for participating in the consensus reality in an acceptable way, and they have an enormous number of external and internalized prohibitions that keep them from thinking and experiencing in ways not approved by the consensus reality.

Conventional, culture-based religion is largely an enterprise of childhood of the dependent, childish state. When people become adults, however, they have more hard facts to deal with in life. They feel much less protected than they did as children in the household of their parents. So they begin to question and to doubt the existence of this Parental Deity. Such individuals may continue to be conventionally religious in some sense, willing to play the game of social morality and good behaviour, but they carry on a rather adolescent relationship of dependence-independence, or embrace and withdrawal, relative to this 'God-Person'. Atheism is the ultimate form of denial of the Parental God. Atheism is not founded on real observation of the ultimate facts of the universe. Rather, it is a kind of adolescent development of the human species. What characterises the doctrine or dogma of atheism is not a discovery that there is no God, but a refusal to acknowledge every kind of parent or parent-like authority, including, therefore, the Parental God of childish culture.

All of the philosophical religious conundrums about whether God exists or not are simply a continuation of the doubting and subjective problem of separate existence or consciousness that is part of the adolescence of humankind. Wondering about whether God exists is simply an occupation of basically adolescent personalities whose notions of God were formed by the childhood situation of dependence. Thus, wondering about whether God exists is basically an effort to prove the existence of the God believed in as a child. Nevertheless, the God believed in as a child does not exist, not as it was then described, nor as believed.

The Parental God of childish cultures cannot be proven to exist because that kind of separate God does not exist. The struggle to prove the existence of such a one is a false struggle. It is an expression of the common problem: consciousness of a threatened self that is separate from true reality. The God who truly exists is not present as a separate or exclusively other. He can only be the only true existence beyond any limited cultural concepts and desires.

Uniscape

Haqqiqa means the Reality, this derives from the Divine Name, the Real. *Haqq* is both the Essence of Allah, because He is One in His acts and attributes and essence and He is also that from which the whole phenomenal world manifests. Existent reality is by *Haqq*.

The Real is the non-spatial reality on which the time-space dual zone is dependent. Man is the interspace, or between these two realities. The human being, in his or her outwardness, has access to the universal realities of the cosmos. In inwardness, he or she has access to his or her own reality in the unseen worlds.

What the Qur'an unfolds is the secret that man's outwardness is the cosmos, so that the total cosmic reality is one identity, one selfhood, whereas the inwardness of man is what contains the plenum of cosmic outwardness. It is the cosmos that you understand by going inward, whereas it is the self you understand by going outward. Unity of these two knowledges is arrived at by pushing the central locus of awareness out of dimensionality, until locus itself is shattered. This happens by going beyond the universal unitary reality, into the void, the original void that was before the cosmic Big Bang. Until man makes the inward journey, he does not understand the cosmos.

Beyond the void lies the goal of the seeker by which he faces his unity, *Tawhid*, and understands that He is indeed the Outwardly Manifest and the Inwardly Hidden.

> Another name that fairly describes the goal of Islamic thought is tahqıq. The focus of Muslim intellectuals was not on the practical affairs of this world, but on the full realization of human intelligence. This demanded not only discovering the haqq of things, their truth and reality, but also acting in accordance with that haqq. This could only be determined by

> *reference to al-haqq, the Real, the absolute reality that is God. Tahqıq demands both right thought and right activity, both intellectual perfection and moral perfection.*
> —William Chittick

The human body arises inseparable in the primary field of consciousness. The body itself is a conditionally egoless mechanism of perception and response. There is no separate 'self' inside the body, and the body itself is not a self. The body is an irreducibly complex collection of cooperative mechanisms of perception located in space and time. As the undifferentiated fields of perception come into relationship with one another, the indivisible field is perceived from a location of a body in time and space creating the perception of objects and others. The particularity of objects reflected in and of the body is a perceptual feedback event, which in the body context gives rise to the presumption of a subject or a knowing, separate self.

It is only in this bodily perception-conjunction in which objects arise in consciousness and become reflected in the body perception complex, that a self is psycho-physically presumed to exist as an independent entity.

In summary, it is the event of the phenomenal body relationship with the field of consciousness that naturally becomes the selective perception of arising forms that seems to imply that the body or brain-mind is a separate knowing-self. However, this self is merely a presumption, reflection, or shadow of known-objects. In reality, there is only the selfless arising of events and objects, including our bodies, in the dimensionless field of consciousness.

In truth, my bodily self is the intersection of time and eternity, of being and becoming.

> *Identification is that effect of conditioning whereby a shadow is taken for its substance, the source of the shadow, and all they both are, whether united or apparently separated in the dimensions of space. It might almost be possible to say that not only is shadow taken for substance, but also that substance—if cognized at all—is taken for shadow. But a shadow has no*

8 - The View of the Biosphere

life of its own, nor any nature, character, or attribute; all it is lies in its source, of which it is a phenomenal reflection, deformed, partial, limited to two dimensions, constantly in flux, and utterly devoid of entity, an abstraction, an 'appearance' illusorily separated from its own substance. However, everything the shadow appears to do, its every manifestation, as it is perceived is not performed by its substance but is an objectified representation of some movement on the part of that source.
—*Wei Wu Wei*

What is this 'I'? You will, on close introspection, find that what you really mean by 'I' is the ground-stuff upon which experiences and memories are collected.
—*Erwin Schrödinger*

First he appeared in the realm inanimate;
Thence came into the world of plants and lived
The plant-life many a year, nor called to mind
What he had been; then took the onward way

To animal existence, and once more
Remembers naught of what life vegetive,
Save when he feels himself moved with desire
Towards it in the season of sweet flowers,

As babes that seek the breast and know not why.
Again the wise Creator whom thou knowest
Uplifted him from animality
To Man's estate; and so from realm to realm

Advancing, he became intelligent,
Cunning and keen of wit, as he is now.
No memory of his past abides with him,
And from his present soul he shall be changes

Though he is fallen asleep, God will not leave him

LIGHTS OF CONSCIOUSNESS

In this forgetfulness. Awakened, he
Will laugh to think what troublous dreams he had.
And wonder how his happy state of being

He could forget, and not perceive that all
Those pains and sorrows were the effect of sleep
And guile and vain illusion. So this world
Seems lasting, though 'tis but the sleepers' dream;
Who, when the appointed Day shall dawn, escapes
From dark imaginings that haunted him,
And turns with laughter on his phantom griefs
When he beholds his everlasting home.
                              —Rumi

9 - The View of Philosophy

He gives the wisdom to whomsoever He will, and whoso is given the wisdom, has been given much good; yet none remembers but men possessed of the kernel.
—Qur'an 2.269

I am a wanderer and mountain climber he said to his heart. I do not like the plains, and it seems I cannot sit still for long. And whatever may yet come to me as fate and experience, a wandering and a mountain climbing will be in it: in the final analysis one experiences only oneself.
—Friedrich Nietzsche

The Quest for Meaning

The word *philosophy* comes from the Greek word *philosophia*, which means love of wisdom, it is the study of general and fundamental problems, such as those connected with existence, knowledge, values, reason, mind and language. Originally, what we now call science was termed *natural philosophy*: that branch that is concerned with studying the natural world, distinct from the sciences of humanities.

Our cosmology is a personal philosophical worldview: core beliefs that we espouse about the universe and ourselves, and the frame of reference by which we interpret and understand life. *Ontology*, the philosophy of being, concerns itself with the ultimate nature of existence.

Aristotle was the first philosopher who systematically studied, recorded and criticized the work of previous philosophers. In his first book of the *Metaphysics*, he summarises the teachings of his predecessors, starting from his distant intellectual ancestors like Pythagoras and Thales up to Plato, his teacher for 20 years.

Aristotle offers a classification of the earliest Greek philosophers in accordance with the structure of his system of the four causes. Scientific inquiry, he believed, was above all inquiry into the causes of things, and there were four different kinds of causes: the material cause, the efficient cause, the formal cause, and the final cause. Here is an illustration of what he had in mind: When we cook a meal, the material causes of the meal are the ingredients that go into it, the efficient cause is the chef him- or herself, the recipe is the formal cause, and the satisfaction of consumption is the final cause.

Early philosophers on the Greek coast of Asia Minor concentrated on the material cause, in that they sought the basic ingredients of the world we live in. Thales and his successors posed the following question: At a fundamental level, is the world made out of water, or air, or fire, or earth, or a combination of some or all of these?

Even if we have an answer to this question, Aristotle thought, that was clearly not enough to satisfy our scientific curiosity. The ingredients of a dish do not put themselves together. There needs to be an agent operating upon them, by cutting, mixing, stirring, heating, or the like.

Some of these early philosophers, Aristotle tells us, were aware of this and offered conjectures about the agents of change and development in the world. Sometimes it would be one of the ingredients themselves that was perhaps the most promising suggestion, as being the least torpid of the elements. More often it would be some agent, or pair of agents, both more abstract and more picturesque, such as Love or Desire or Strife, or the Good and the Bad.

Meanwhile in Italy, according to Aristotle, there were, centered around Pythagoras, mathematically inclined philosophers, whose inquiries took quite a different course. A recipe, besides

9 - The View of Philosophy

naming ingredients, will contain a lot of numbers representing quantity, such as grams and litres. The Pythagoreans were more interested in the numbers in the world's recipe rather than in the ingredients themselves. They supposed, Aristotle says, that the elements of numbers were the elements of all things, and the whole of the heavens was a musical scale. They were inspired in their quest by their discovery that the relationship between the notes of the scale played on a lyre corresponded to different numerical ratios between the lengths of the strings. They then generalized this idea that qualitative differences might be the upshot of numerical differences. Their inquiry, in Aristotle's terms, was an inquiry into the formal causes of the universe.

Coming to his immediate predecessors, Aristotle says that Socrates preferred to concentrate on ethics rather than study the world of nature, whereas Plato in his philosophical theory combined the approaches of the schools of both Thales and Pythagoras. But Plato's Theory of Ideas, althouth being the most comprehensive scientific system yet devised, seemed to Aristotle—for reasons that he summarises here and develops in a number of his treatises—to be unsatisfactory on several grounds.

There were so many things to explain, Aristotle said, and the Ideas just added new items calling for explanation. They did not provide a solution; they added to the problem. Aristotle's agenda was to show how previous philosophers neglected the remaining member of the quartet of causes—the final cause—which was to play a most significant role in his own philosophy of nature.

The fact is that the distinction between religion, science, and philosophy was not as clear as it became in later centuries. The works of Aristotle and his master Plato provide a paradigm of philosophy for every age, and to this day anyone using the title 'philosopher' is claiming to be one of their heirs.

The history of philosophy bears evidence that neither the concept of non-change nor change is adequate to fully describe the nature of being. Exclusive emphasis on immutability leads to the denial of the world and our very sense of self as an individual viewing them as an illusion. Exclusive emphasis on change and difference divides reality, creating an unbridgeable gap between man and God.

Parmenides suggested that all change was an illusion. Reality consist of one simple, complete and eternal being. He insisted that we could say nothing sensible about phenomena that did not exist. Because being was eternal and not subject to alteration, there was no such thing as change.

It appears that creatures come into being and pass away, Aristotle said, but this is an illusion because reality is beyond time and change. He cultivated the habit of reflection upon the thought processes themselves. He had arrived at a new critical awareness of the limitations of human knowledge. He embarked on the philosophical quest for pure existence. Instead of contemplating individual creatures, he was trying to put his finger on quintessential being. But in the process, he created a world in which it was impossible to live. By divesting the cosmos of qualities, he had also deprived it of heart.

Heraclites was the first relativist who said that everything depended on context. The universe is in constant flux and a battlefield of warring elements. Yet beneath this cosmic turbulence, he said, there was unity. Flux and stability, which are antithetical, seem to suggest that we are one and the same thing and that night and day were two sides of the same coin. You could not rely on the evidence of your senses, but must look deeper to find the *logos*, the ruling principle of nature. In this way, he discovered introspection.

Both concepts at the same time seem necessary: Inasmuch as essential identity is a necessary demand of our reason, difference is an undeniable fact of our experience. Therefore a synthesis of the two can be seen as the goal of philosophy. In a complete theory the concepts of both Oneness and difference are transcended and reconciled in this higher synthesis, and thus they become associated aspects of an abiding unity in the Godhead.

The realisation that we do not experience reality as it is, but only a picture of reality constructed in the mind, is not new. In *The Republic*, Plato argued that the objects we perceive are not the ultimate reality, but more like a shadow of reality. He illustrated this with his analogy of the Cave.

A group of people, living in an underground cave, are forced

9 - The View of Philosophy

to sit with their backs to the entrance. All they can see is the far wall of the cave. In the mouth of the cave is a large fire, and between the fire and the backs of the people, parade various creatures, whose shadows are cast by the fire onto the cave wall. The prisoners in the cave cannot turn their heads to see the creatures. All they can see are the flickering shadows on the wall in front of them. Because this is all they have seen since the day they were born, they think these shadows are all that exist.

In Plato's story, one of the prisoners manages to free himself, and, looking around, realises that everything he took to be reality is but a shadow. Outside he finds the true world of colour and three-dimensional forms. Overjoyed with his discovery, he returns to his former companions to tell them the good news. But try as he may, he cannot convince them that everything they see in only flickering shadows of the 'real world'. In the end, the other prisoners kill him rather than accept such a nonsensical notion.

Although Plato believed the real world was a world of ideas and eternal perfect forms, his story is still pertinent to our own experience. Most of us assume that the sights and sounds we perceive are the 'real world'. When science informs us that we are not seeing reality as it is, but merely the images that manifest in our minds, we shrug in disbelief. How can that be? How can the world that I experience so clearly, as 'out there', be just an image in the mind?

> *Man's search for meaning is the primary motivation in his life and not a 'secondary rationalisation' of instinctual drives. This meaning is unique and specific in that it must and can be fulfilled by him alone; only then does it achieve a significance which will satisfy his own will to meaning*
> —*Viktor Frankl*

NOUMENON

The notion that reality is 'all in the mind' resurfaces repeatedly in modern philosophy. The person who is generally regarded as having made the greatest contributions in this area is the eighteenth-century German philosopher Immanuel Kant. Building on the work of Bishop Berkeley and John Locke, Kant drew a clear distinction between our perception of reality and the actual object of perception. His key insight was the realisation that all we ever know is the structures generated in our minds. The world that gives rise to this perception, what he termed 'the thing-in-itself', remains forever unknowable.

Kant's ideas did not arise out of nowhere. The groundwork for his thinking had been laid by others. Locke, British philosopher, had argued a century before that all knowledge is based on perceptions produced by the action of external objects on the senses. But whereas Locke thought this was a passive process—the mind simply receiving the sense impressions—Kant proposed that the mind is a participant in the process, actively shaping our experience of the world.

Unlike some of his predecessors, Kant was not saying that there is nothing apart from what exists in the mind. Berkeley had, some 50 years before, argued that we know only what we perceive, and had then concluded that only that which we perceive exists. The only reality is that experienced in the mind. This led him into the difficult position of having to explain what happened to the world when no one perceived it, which he tried to resolve by arguing that it was being observed in the mind of God. Kant's position was that there is an underlying reality that correlates with our experience, but exactly what this underlying reality is, we can never know.

All we can ever know, proposed Kant, is how reality appears to us, what he referred to as the phenomenon of our experience, 'that which appears to be'. The underlying reality he called the *noumenon*, a Greek word meaning 'that which is apprehended', the thing perceived.

Kant's statement that the noumenon is forever unknowable should be interpreted as forever inexperiencable. The mind is forever barred from a direct knowing of the thing-in-itself. This does not imply that we cannot understand it, or form concepts about it, which is what modern science sets out to do.

Because all we ever know is the product of the mind operat-

9 - The View of Philosophy

ing on the raw sensory data, Kant reasoned that our experience is as much a reflection of the nature of the mind as it is of the physical world. This led him to one of his boldest, and at that time most astonishing, conclusions of all. Time and space, he argued, are not inherent qualities of the physical world; they are a reflection of the way the mind operates, the perceptual framework within which our entire experience of the world is constructed.

It seems absolutely obvious to us that time and space are real and fundamental qualities of the physical world, entirely independent of my or your consciousness, as obvious as it seemed to people 500 years ago that the Sun moves round the Earth. This, said Kant, is only because we cannot see the world any other way. The human mind is so constituted that it is forced to impose the framework of space and time on the raw sensory data in order to make any sense of it at all. We are forever constrained to construct our experience within these dimensions, much as a computer is forever constrained to present its data in the two-dimensional format of the monitor. It is a law of perception rather than a law of physics.

It may have been an astonishing claim at the time, and it is probably still undeniable that the world we experience extends out there around us, but it is a realisation that contemporary physics is just coming around to accepting.

At the time, Kant's arguments were a leap in Western thinking. They were, as Kant himself saw, the equivalent of a Copernican Revolution in philosophy. Whereas Nicolaus Copernicus had effectively turned the physical universe inside out, showing that the movements of the stars are determined by the movement of the Earth, Kant had turned the epistemological world inside out. We are not passive experiencers of the world; we are the creators of the world we experience. He had put the self firmly at the centre of things.

Later, another German philosophe, Georg W. F. Hegel developed a theory of evolving consciousness. According to Hegel, the Absolute is Spirit and Spirit is Reality. All truth is within the Absolute. The Absolute has self-existence; it has being-for-itself. Hegel declares that the essential reality of that which has being-for-itself is not in an other. The other is not essential to that which has being-for-itself.

The essential reality of that which has being-for-itself is self-existence. The Absolute is being in-and-for-itself and it is thus an absolute negation of otherness. Hegel describes consciousness as developing through 'moments' (stages) that include sense-certainty, perception and understanding. Sense-certainty is an experience of the immediacy of sensation, which does not depend on either the subject or object. Perception is awareness that an object is universal and unconditioned by sensation. Understanding is recognition that the unconditioned universality of the true object of consciousness transcends sensation and perception.

According to Hegel, the world of appearances is directly perceived, but the world of inherent being is not directly perceived. The 'sensible' world is the antithesis of the 'supersensible' world. But both worlds are aspects of the same reality. Mind is absolute substance, and the concept of Mind is found by the self in self-consciousness. Self-consciousness may be in-itself, for-itself, or for-another. The self-consciousness that is in-itself is an object for itself, or for another. The self-consciousness that is for-itself is independent. The self-consciousness that is for-another is dependent.

Hegel sees the relation between independent and dependent self-consciousness as similar to the relation between lordship and bondage, or between master and slave. The master is independent of being determined by an 'other.' The slave is dependent on being determined by an 'other.' The consciousness of the 'other' is unessential to independent self-consciousness, but the consciousness of the 'other' is a determining factor for dependent self-consciousness.

Self-consciousness has otherness within itself insofar as the self is conscious of what is other than itself. But this 'other' is unessential to self-consciousness. Self-consciousness is contradictory when it is conscious of both sameness and otherness. This divided mode of consciousness is what Hegel calls the 'unhappy consciousness'. When unity is not present between independent and dependent self-consciousness, the self is in conflict with itself. This 'unhappy consciousness' is conscious of itself as being divided and as not being able to reconcile itself with the 'other'. On the other hand, the undivided consciousness is a dual self-consciousness that brings unity to the self and the 'other.'

Consciousness is described by Hegel as being both active and passive. Passivity can be sublated by activity. Activity can be sublated by passivity. According to Hegel, Force is a process that can move consciousness actively or passively. Force proper is the process whereby individual elements of consciousness are assembled into an undivided unity. On the other hand, the expression of Force may disperse individual elements into greater disunity. Force may have moments (stages) of expression or withdrawal. The interplay of the two opposing moments of Force may be mediated by Understanding, which brings the two opposing moments into a single undivided unity. Thus, Force is the process that moves consciousness to an Understanding that unconditioned universality is the inner being of all things.

Hegel describes Reason as self-consciousness, and self-consciousness as Reason. Self-consciousness becomes all reality, as the evolving dialectical triad of Intention (the thesis), Perception (the antithesis), and Understanding (the synthesis) demonstrates that otherness is not inherently real. Reason belongs to the Absolute in that Reason is the conscious certainty of being all reality. The Absolute is a universal reality that is absolutely conscious of itself.

According to Hegel, all reality is Reason. Whatever is real is rational, and whatever is rational is real. The reality of Reason has a universal necessity. Whatever is irrational cannot have a conscious certainty of its own reality. Reason is also seen in the unfolding of the World-Spirit. Reason is aware of itself as spirit and of spirit as real. The World-Spirit determines its own reality as it develops into self-consciousness. Reason is a unity of self and other, of subjectivity and objectivity, of being-for-itself and being-in-itself. Reason is aware of itself as the ethical world, and it is also a lawgiver for the world of reality.

The separation between the self and the 'other' developing

when the self becomes its own object and becomes an 'other' to itself is described by Hegel as a factor of negativity. The transcendence of this otherness is the attainment of a unified knowledge of substance as spirit, which is the completion of the Phenomenology of Mind. Negativity is a process whereby the self maintains itself within itself, determining itself as an inoperative unity. Negativity is self-existence in otherness. On the other hand, freedom of self-existence is a capacity to establish relationships with other selves in an operative unity. Hegel declares that self-consciousness is an essential reality to itself as individual Mind. Self-consciousness is aware of itself as essentially real and as expressing its own individuality. Thus, the ethical world establishes the absolute spiritual unity of individuals in their independent reality. Hegel argues that although pure individuality may be the antithesis of pure universality, the self in its 'heart' may feel their immediate unity. The self may realise that self-existence is necessary and universal. Thus, the 'law of the heart' produces a 'universal individuality.' The World Process is, by nature, real and universal, but individuality is the actualisation of this universal reality.

For Hegel, spirituality produces the ethical life of the world. Spiritual individualities are unifying forms of the ethical world. The conscious activity by which individual forms of spirit return to the self of spirit is the process by which Absolute Spirit becomes itself and has its reality.

> *We must realize that thoughts are not merely a reflection on reality, but are also a movement of that very reality itself. Thought is a performance of that which it seeks to know, and not a simple mirror of something unrelated to itself. The mapmaker, the self, the thinking and knowing subject, is actually a product and a performance of that which it seeks to know and represent.*
> —Georg W. F. Hegel

> *'Noumenon' necessarily is total potentiality. If it functions, in functioning it must be subjective, and thereby inevitably*

9 - The View of Philosophy

objective also. That is to say, subject objectivises itself and so becomes apparent to itself as object, manifesting phenomenally 'within' itself. It looks at itself and perceives the universe—which is then apparently outside itself, since objectivisation is a process of apparent exteriorisation. Therefore the phenomenal universe is the objective aspect of noumenon. Phenomena, therefore, are not something projected by noumenon: they are the appearance of noumenon, or noumenon rendered objective and apparent.

—Wei Wu Wei

Non-duality

The central position of the Advaita Vedanta, one of the main philosophical systems of India, is that in reality there is no difference between consciousness and the universe, no real distinction between the individual, the entire universe. and God, Brahman. Advaita (meaning 'not two' or non-dual) declares that the universe is a manifestation of one undifferentiated reality, expressed in Sanskrit as *Brahman* which means 'growth', 'development', or the 'Supreme transcendent and immanent Reality or the One Godhead'.

Shankara, one of Advaita's greatest exponents, describes the nature of Brahman as that which permeates all, which nothing transcends, and which, like the universal space around us, fills everything completely from within and without, that Supreme non-dual Brahman—that thou art.

At the heart of its philosophical system, Advaita rests on the personal experience of a non-dual state of being. Here, one's normal sense of a distinction between the subject and the object is experienced as non-existent. All forms, whether another person, a bird, a sight, a sound, a thought, or a feeling become part and parcel of one's very awareness, a spontaneous manifestation of that awareness.

This experience lies at the heart of Advaita and forms the foundation upon which both its practice and thought is referred to, along with other non-dual traditions, such as Zen. Advaita sets forward several transpersonal ('beyond just a personal or individual sense of self') states of individual development leading up to the experience of non-duality.

Advaita suggests that in the ultimate analysis, that is, in full 'moksha' or liberation from the limited sense of self the world is experienced as non-dual, it also fully recognises that we normally experience life in terms of duality. Given that Advaita puts forward a non-dual field of existence as the ground to the universe and also as the ground and basis of human experience, it then suggests that we are in a sense dreaming or are under the influence of life's grandest illusion or *maya* as it is termed in Sanskrit. Just as we dream at night, or even during a particularly exciting part of the day, where we are someone else, somewhere else doing, something else, Advaita suggests we are dreaming right now. We are dreaming that we are a fairly small individual, entirely separate and isolated from everything and everybody else, when in fact we are entirely connected, related, and integrated with every other creature, atom, and element in this grand cosmos. The world of duality is said to be a superimposition upon the non-dual Brahman.

Consciousness is used extensively in reference to Brahman, both in the absolute sense of limitless Consciousness and the relative sense of pure awareness, or the eternal knower who watches all the many forms of knowledge and the objects of knowledge. From the relative perspective, it is expressed as the eternal thread untouched by phenomena, a thread used to negate and detach from the duality arising in mind.

The process of negating or detaching one's attachment from whatever arises in one's perception is one of the key practices of Advaita: 'neti, neti', or 'not this, not this', the sense being that one is not 'limited' by the thoughts that arise in the mind, nor the feelings in the heart, nor the sensations of the body, but that one's sense of self is founded on the pure witnessing consciousness, untouched by any objects of awareness. When there is a full sense of freedom from these objects (not that they disappear, but that they do not define and limit one's sense of being in the slightest), the awareness seems to expand, become heightened and be completely

9 - The View of Philosophy

blissful, in and of its self, for no reason other than that it seems to be a part of its very nature: infinite and blissful.

Traditionally Advaita Vedanta describes four basic levels of reality, reflected in both the macrocosm and microcosm. It is often described in different ways, but the fourfold structure is the most basic expressed throughout many traditions. The four are:

1. Physical world;
2. Subtle;
3. Causal; and
4. Nirguna or Brahman, which is the non-dual ground of the other three.

Each greater structure transcends and includes the others, in infinite shades, from quark, atom, cell, and molecule up to Brahman itself.

Within the individual these four structures, if the last one can really be called a 'structure' at all, are experienced as individual levels of consciousness. These structures support the individual sense of self, and in themselves they appear to be devoid of an inherent self-sense; therefore the self can identify with any of them. That is, one of the primary characteristics of the self seems to be its capacity to identify with the basic structures or levels of consciousness, and every time it does so, according to this view, it generates a specific type of self-identity, with specific needs and drives.

Within the mental, subtle and causal levels of consciousness are some of the meditative stages mentioned previously as well as the conventional stages of psychological growth. The individual at each level exhibits a different worldview and different subject-object relationship. This relationship becomes finer and finer as the 'self' transcends each structure, until the distinction is eventually seen to be unreal.

Within the nature of the individual, Advaita Vedanta makes a distinction, just as a distinction has been made in knowledge. On one hand, there is the individual's essential nature identical with Brahman, commonly referred to as Pure Consciousness or as the pure sense of 'I am' ness (*Aham*). On the other hand, there is the 'self', the individual personality. The 'self' is described as a limiting adjunct (*upadhi*) upon the undivided nature of Consciousness. Thus within the individual, Pure Consciousness or the sense of I Am-ness (*Aham*) is co-joined and limited to some form in the world. Therefore you have *Ahankara* (I Am *Aham* + Creation/world [kara] = I am a human). This sense of individuality relies upon the superimposition of various thoughts, objects and perceptions onto Pure Consciousness. However, when deconstructed and negated, as in meditative practice, the real nature immediately manifests itself.

Thus the crux of Advaita is not only the realisation that the limited 'self' is ultimately unreal, but that the sense of personal identity, the 'ego', is in fact primarily based upon the constant and continual sense of Consciousness that we all feel in its many varied forms and expressions at all times. Advaita maintains that this Consciousness is self-luminous, only revealing itself fully as limitless and blissful when stripped of all other limiting mental adjuncts.

> *You are the Self, the infinite Being, the pure, unchanging Consciousness, which pervades everything. Your nature is bliss and your glory is without stain. Because you identify yourself with the ego, you are tied to birth and death. Your bondage has no other cause.*
> —Adi Shankara

Gnostic *Hikma*

In Islam, wisdom, *hikma* is structurally a peculiar combination of rational thinking and Gnostic intuition, or, we might say, rationalist philosophy and mystical experience. It is a special type of scholastic philosophy based on existential intuition of Reality, a result of philosophising the Gnostic ideas and visions obtained through intellectual contemplation. With regard to the second aspect of the wisdom just distinguished, namely, the fact that a mystical or Gnostic experience underlies the whole structure of its philosophy, wisdom is not an outcome of mere intellectual labor on the level of reason. It is, rather, an original product of the

9 - The View of Philosophy

activity of keen analytic reason combined with, and backed by, a profound intuitive grasp of reality, or even of something beyond that kind of reality that is accessible to human consciousness.

> *The Islamic quest for wisdom was always a quest to achieve unity with the Divine light or the Divine spirit. By the nature of the quest, Muslim intellectuals knew from the outset that everything had come from the One and will return to the One. Their quest was not to 'believe' that God is one, because they already knew that God is one. The unity of Ultimate Reality was too self-evident to be doubted. The quest was to understand the implications of unity thoroughly and completely.*
> —William Chittick

The sixteenth century Muslim philosopher and Gnostic Sadrudin Shirazi, also known as Mulla Sadra, stated that 'knowledge is neither a privation like abstraction from matter nor a relation but a being or a mode of existence'. In Mulla Sadra's view, the act of knowing involves a transformation of the being of the self of the knower when it comes into contact with a mode of existence. Knowledge of something is the creation of the intelligible form of that thing by the knower.

The self, as a cognising element, cannot receive a form that is not of a similar nature or mode of existence as itself. For Mulla Sadra, perceptible forms are not externally existent forms but are emanations or creations of the human self. Objective material objects cannot be presented to the mind as they are and therefore become known by the perceiver. The human self has to create a form that is of a similar nature to itself and that corresponds to the perceived object. Perception is only a preparatory stage that provides the occasion for the self to create a form of the perceptible object. For Mulla Sadra, all intelligible forms are produced by the self in this way.

If, in the case of sense perception, the senses mediate between the external object and the act of perception, in relation to imagination and intellect, there are no sense organs that are employed in the creation of their intelligible forms. Because the nature of the self is existence, the knowledge it receives or acquires must also be existence. The knower and the known must be identical, and knowledge must arise from self-identity or direct intuition.

In order for a subject to know an object, it must possess the intelligible form of the object concerned, which corresponds to the form of the object, but the existence of the form must belong to the same mode of existence as the soul. The form of the known object is transformed from the level of material or external existence to that of mental existence by the self of the knower. Therefore, the self must create a form that not only corresponds to the form of the known object but also to its own mode of existence. The external object cannot be known directly by the self, but the intelligible form of the object, which is of a mental existence, can be known directly by the subject. The rational self cannot be united with external objects, but it can be united with the intelligible forms, which are incorporeal and insensible and, like itself, are independent of matter.

When the self creates an intelligible form within itself, that which is known becomes transformed from the state of potentiality to actuality and the self too becomes transformed from a knower in potentiality to a knower in actuality. Correspondingly, knowledge has emerged from potentiality to actuality. It is through the intellectual form that the knower in potentiality becomes a knower in actuality. The intellectual form becomes the 'eye' of the self by which it sees the object of its knowledge, as well as the image of that which it sees. Thus, the perceiving subject, or the knower, and the perceived object, or the known, are identical.

The Necessary Being, which is the philosophical term for God, is defined as one whose Essence is inseparable from or identical with its Being. The Being of God is conceived of as identical to Its Essence and Its Essence is identified with Its Being. The Necessary Being is considered to be self-subsistent and metaphysically necessary, and all the possible beings of the universe are regarded as metaphysically contingent upon it.

According to Mulla Sadra, the Necessary Being knows of his essence, and he is the Necessary Being whose essence is identical with his being, knowledge in God implies a unity between

9 - The View of Philosophy

the subject who knows, the object that is known and the Act of knowing. In other words, God is at once the Knower, the Known and Knowledge.

Creation, or the manifestation of existents by the Necessary Being, is the result of his contemplation of his essence. It is his contemplation or knowledge of his own essence that brings forth all things into existence. Because being and knowledge are identical in God, God's knowledge brings beings or existents. In God, to know of a thing is also to confer existence to that thing which is known by him. Therefore, the beings of things are identified as God's very knowledge of them and God's knowledge constitutes the substance of cosmic manifestation. God's knowledge of the essence or form of a thing leads to the objective existence of that particular form. God's contemplation of his essence is infinite, and the manifestation of the universe constitutes God's eternal knowledge of himself.

Mulla Sadra's theory that reality and existence are identical also states that existence is one but graded in intensity. To this graded intensity he gave the name *tashkik al-wujud*, which has been translated as the 'systematic ambiguity' of existence. This enabled him to say that it is the same existence that occurs in all things, but that existential instances differ in terms of 'priority and posteriori, perfection and imperfection, strength and weakness'. He was thus able to explain that it was pure existence alone that had the property of combining 'unity in multiplicity and multiplicity in unity'.

Reality is therefore pure existence, but it is an existence that manifests itself in different modes, and it is these modes that present themselves in the mind. Even the term 'in the mind', however, is merely an expression denoting a particular mode of being, that of mental existence, albeit an extremely attenuated mode. Everything is thus comprehended by existence, even 'nothingness', which must on being conceived assume the most meagre portion of existence in order to become a mental existent. When reality, or, rather, a mode of existence presents, itself to the mind, the mind abstracts an essence from it—being unable, except in exceptional circumstances, to grasp existence intuitively—and in the mind the essence becomes, as it were, the reality and existence, the accident. However, this 'existence' that the mind predicates of the essence is itself merely a notion or concept, one of the secondary intelligibles.

Mulla Sadra considers man as a microcosm who is composed of all the various degrees or levels of cosmic existence. For Mulla Sadra, the being, like God, knows of things through the contemplation or intellection of the intelligible forms of things latent in his soul. If God's knowledge or contemplation of the form of a thing leads to its objective existence, then the human's knowledge or intellection of the form of a thing leads to its mental existence. When a human knows of the form of a thing, that form is present in his soul. When God knows the form of a thing, that form is given existence or presence in the external world. Therefore, God's knowledge of the forms of things manifest, them in the external world and they are bestowed with objective existence, and the human being's knowledge of the forms of things manifests them and gives them mental existence.

Both God and man possess the creative power of manifesting forms. However, God is Pure Being, His creation involves real existence, and because the human being is a contingent being, he can only create forms within the limits of the reality or intensity of his being.

Therefore, for Mulla Sadra, the relation of the intelligible forms to the human soul is analogous to the relation of the contingent beings to the Necessary Being. Human knowledge and the act of knowing are founded on the Divine model.

The goal of Mulla Sadra's doctrine of the intellect is to show that the human mind ultimately unites itself with the Active Intelligence or the Universal Intellect. Because, according to Mulla Sadra, the end of all substantive essential movement is to achieve a new level of being, knowledge represents, for him, such substantive movement whose end is the union of the human intellect with the transcendent intellect and hence the achievement of a new level of existence—that of pure, simple intellect. Further, because this evolutionary movement is cumulative, it represents something positive, inclusive of the lower levels of being and not excluding or negating them. This means that which exists at the lower levels with separate or mutually exclusive parts exists at the higher levels as mutually inclusive and unitary.

Mulla Sadra classifies knowledge into acquired knowledge and knowledge by presence. He categorises the knowledge by presence into three classes: knowledge of soul to itself, knowledge of cause to its effect and knowledge of effect to its cause.

The acquired knowledge, or the knowledge of human soul of something other than itself, is not the mere reflection of the forms of objects in the soul. Rather, the human soul has a creative power similar to that of the Divine creative power and can create the forms in the soul. These forms depend upon the soul as the external world depends upon the essence of the Truth.

Knowledge by presence is the direct perception of objective reality, which is restricted to the immaterial being's knowledge of its own essences and states, the sufficient cause's knowledge of its own effect, and the mortal being's knowledge of what happens within it. Acquired knowledge, however, is the reception of the image of objective reality and not that reality itself.

> *To stand alone is to be uncorrupted, innocent, free of all tradition, of dogma, of opinion, of what another says, and so on. Such a mind does not seek because there is nothing to seek; being free, such a mind is completely still without a want, without movement. But this state is not to be achieved; it isn't a thing that you buy through discipline; it doesn't come into being by giving up sex, or practicing a certain yoga. It comes into being only when there is understanding of the ways of the self, the 'me', which shows itself through the conscious mind in everyday activity, and also in the unconscious. What matters is to understand for oneself, not through the direction of others, the total content of consciousness, which is conditioned, which is the result of society, of religion, of various impacts, impressions, memories—to understand all that conditioning and be free of it. But there is no 'how' to be free. If you ask how to be free, you are not listening.*
> —Jiddu Krishnamurti

10 - The View of Self

Mankind, revere your Lord, who created you of a single self, and from it created its mate, and from the pair of them scattered abroad many men and women; and revere Allah by whom you demand one of another, and the wombs; surely Allah ever watches over you.
—Qur'an 4.1

Every experience is real at the time of its occurrence. Experienced realities, however, are all relative and change according to subjective perceptions and evaluations.
The same event may be interpreted differently by different people at different times.
As our 'subjective' interpretations become subtle and refined our reading becomes more 'real' and the 'truth' behind each reality becomes evident.
This is the difference between human view and judgment from the underlying truth.
Human justice and laws can change whereas Divine natural laws are perpetual and constant.
Good and bad are relative in human terms whereas what is always good is that which will lead to knowledge of Truth.
—Shaykh Fadhlalla Haeri

The subject yearns for and at the same time is terrified of real transcendence, because transcendence entails the 'death' of his isolated and separate self-sense. The subject can find the prior whole only by letting go of the boundary between subject and object, that is by dying to the exclusive subject. And because he can't or won't let go of and die to his separate self, he cannot

find true and real transcendence, he cannot find the larger fulfillment as the whole. Holding on to himself, his subjectivity, he shuts out his soul, grasping only his own ego, he denies the rest of the All.
—Ken Wilber

To the degree that I believe in the reality of 'the other' Am I removed from my own reality.
—Ghalib

Basic Sketch

In the simplest understanding, the self-anatomy is composed of three fundamental dimensions, which can be defined as gross, subtle and source, or outer, inner and essence. The gross (or outer) dimension corresponds to the physical level of experience and the waking state. The subtle (or inner) dimension includes everything to do with mind, emotion, and energy, including the domain of dreaming and psychic experience, as well as the range of supernormal experience that is commonly called 'mystical'. The essential dimension refers to the depth where the 'I'-'other' sense originates, thereby 'causing', or generating, the worlds of subtle and gross experience that extend from that root presumption of separate identity.

Exoteric religion is strictly an outer, waking-state affair, motivated by the concerns of physical existence. Whatever its particular characteristics of doctrine and practice in any time and place, exoteric religion is a search for consolation and salvation through belief in some kind of "Creator God" or patron deity, and an adherence to a moral code of behaviour that promotes social order.

The esoteric traditions, accounting for a small minority of humanity's religious endeavours, conduct a more refined and inward form of seeking. They aspire to transcend the common myths and Awaken directly to what is ultimate. They all speak, in one way or another, of realising an ultimate source-condition of the impermanent, arising world.

10 - The View of Self

The esoteric sciences are focused either in the subtle dimension, which is the realm of the various mystical and yogic traditions, or in the essential or soul dimension, which is the domain of the sages, the masters who are exclusively invested in knowing the Transcendental Reality. Thus, the esoteric traditions of humankind have been polarised around these two different orientations—the orientation to subtle energy and light as the means and nature of Realisation on the one hand, and the urge to Realise Consciousness, independent of objects, on the other.

A science of the self is a fully developed model or map of the progressive developmental potential of the human being, based on its total psycho-physical structure—outer, inner and essence. What has traditionally been called the ego can be understood to be an activity, or, more correctly, a re-activity—activity of self-contraction, a recoil or a re-action in conscious awareness. From this ego-act stems all our notions about reality. We see an apparent world of separate beings and things from a point of awareness that we call 'I'. This is the world we presume to live in, the world we think is real. But it is real only from a limited 'point of view'. And it is not a 'free' world. It is a world fraught with the bondage of frenetic seeking, the never-ending search to overcome the core ego-stress that is our fundamental, self-created world of suffering.

> *You will notice that the separate-self (or ego) simply arises in consciousness like everything else. You can actually feel the self-contraction, just as you can feel your legs, or feel a table, or feel a rock, or feel your feet. The self-contraction is a feeling of interior tension, often localized behind the eyes, and anchored in a slight muscle tension throughout the body mind. It is an effort and a sensation of contracting in the face of the world. It is a subtle whole-body tension.*
> —*Ken Wilber*

Self-contraction is exclusive identification, a binding attention, creating divisions where there is none. The usual human being recoils from the mystery of the infinite by absorption in the reaction of mortal fear. Thus, fear produces self-possession and loss of communion with the Divine. Such recoil produces psycho-physical adaptation of a reactive kind, and every function, every relationship, every condition of experience, high or low in the structure of the body-mind, becomes a reflection of the primal recoil toward self, away from all relations and away from communion with the living mystery that is Divine. The self-possessed individual is wound up in self-recoil, and every part demonstrates the reactive drama of relational avoidance, subjective bondage, and bodily dis-ease.

> *Everyone knows what attention is. It is the taking possession by the mind, in clear and vivid form, of one out of what seem several simultaneously possible objects or trains of thought. Focalization, concentration of consciousness are of its essence. It implies withdrawal from some things in order to deal effectively with others, and is a condition which has a real opposite in the confused, dazed, scatterbrained state.*
> —William James

Based on the understanding of attention or the observation that consciousness Itself, in the context of the body-mind-self, tends to identify with, or becomes fixed in association with, whatever attention observes, and especially with whatever attention surrenders, to most fully, the spiritual motive is essentially the motive to transcend the limiting capability of attention of all conditional objects and states. Therefore, the spiritual effort is an effort to set attention free by progressively relinquishing attachment and reaction to conditional objects, others, states and stations.

Meeting the Mark

To 'sin' is to 'miss the mark'. In Arabic, the term *thanb* clearly signifies the meaning of being off-mark rather than meeting the mark or attaining the heart. It is to be enamoured with things themselves, to have lost the conscious feeling-connection to reality, and to be tuned in to oneself without consciousness. To be

10 - The View of Self

awakened from 'sin' is to meet the mark, that is, to be awakened in consciousness in your heart. Sin is the self-contraction, the presumption of a concretely independent, separate self. It is the act in which the Transcendental Spiritual Divine is simultaneously denied and forgotten. It is the act in which the world, or the total realm of nature, is conceived as a concretely independent, self-contained phenomenal process, without any obvious association with the pervasive Spiritual Being that alone grants reality, security, peace, and happiness to beings and things.

> *Say: O my servants! who have acted extravagantly against their themselves, do not despair of the mercy of Allah; surely Allah covers the faults(sins) altogether; surely He is the concealer, the Merciful.*
> —Qur'an 39.53

Because we actively contract upon the self, we actively separate from, deny, and forget the Divine Being. The action of self-contraction is chronic, complex, and not generally observed or understood. Therefore, the acts of separation, denial, and forgetting relative to the Divine are not commonly observed or understood. (We are simply left with the feeling of un-Happiness, dilemma, the sense of emptiness, or the absence of Profundity, and we are chronically possessed by the urge toward release, or even annihilation.) Such separation, denial, and forgetting are the consequences of self-bondage or sin, but they are not themselves consciously or strategically pursued.

Sin is terrible in itself. Its apparent consequences are merely a reading of what it contains in its very nature. Sin is an act, but it is primarily or instantly shown as a kind of consciousness. As an act, it eventually produces profoundly negative experiential effects, but the act itself immediately coincides with a consciousness, or a state of presumption, that 'designs' the very world un-Reality, so that even what is perceived is no longer recognisable in Truth, as the Divine, Radiant with Bliss. Sin is, therefore, its own 'punishment'. Ultimately, it is not the effects of sin that we must transcend, but sin itself.

Sin is not properly associated with any mythological or collective past, but with the functional individual in the present moment. We are presently performing and suffering this action. We are in a state of present forgetfulness relative to our own Identity and Condition. And we continue to live and act in all relations on the basis of this forgetfulness, which is a consequence of self-contraction.

On the basis of certain traditional religious and social conventions, the idea of sin as the violation of certain behavioural norms or legalisms is developed in the common mind. Therefore, exoteric religious ideas of sin tend to be centred around social and behavioural conceptions of guilt, law, justice, punishment, penance, purification, restitution, moral redress, repentance, forgiveness, salvation from the consequences of wrongdoing, and so forth. Such conceptions are the common psychological basis for traditional social order as well as exoteric religious culture. But sin must ultimately be addressed by Wisdom. Sin is not ultimately a matter of conventional moral transgressions but of Spiritual un-Happiness and the non-Realisation of Truth. We can go on forever 'improving' our behaviours and being punished or forgiven for our presumed wrongdoing, but we will not transcend or go beyond real sin and its ultimate consequences until we observe, understand, and transcend the self-contraction, and so Realise the Spiritual Divine, directly, in Truth, free of the act or the effects of sin.

Self-understanding or realisation is that direct seeing of the fundamental and always present activity that is suffering, ignorance, distraction, motivation, and dilemma. When that activity is most perfectly understood, then there is unconditional realisation of that source which had previously been excluded from conscious awareness, that which is always already present, the Soul. Truth or Reality is a matter of the absence of all contradictions, of every trace of conflict, opposition, division, or desperate motivation, within. In this state beyond all contradiction, it's self-evidently clear that freedom and joy are not attained externally, and are not dependent on any form, object, idea, progress, or experience.

10 - The View of Self

What then is this 'selfhood' that seekers of wisdom were striving to realize? This is the question I now need to address, with the caveat that true and real knowledge of selfhood is inaccessible to any but self. There is no object out there to be known. In knowledge of self, subject and object, knower and known, are the same thing. Moreover, any oral or written expression of self-knowledge can only be received by way of transmission. The only locus of intellectual knowledge is the knowing self. Transmitted expressions can at best point the soul in the right direction.
—*William Chittick*

A Sufi Map

The Sufi path, the Islamic science of the self, considers human beings to be the 'middle people', the inter-space between what seems tangible and what is beyond. All systems of knowledge, all the true prophets and teachers, and every true religion acknowledges this. One aspect of us relates to existential realities on Earth, which have to do with cause and effect, while another keeps us attuned to our origins before time.

The agent of supreme consciousness is the soul that transcends time and space and is also immanent within all of time and space. This is a non-dual mode of consciousness that transcends rational reasoning because its origin is unmanifest and at the same time contains infinite qualities in potentia that manifests as creation.

Creation began from the eternal void, which is referred to as the darkness of non-existence. From this non-existence arises God's Divine Attributes as symbolised by the 99 'most beautiful Names of Allah', and His words.

'If you take all the woods in the world to make pens and take all the oceans as ink, seven times over, My words will not be completed'.
—*Qur'an 31.27*

Manifested creations are the Divine Actions. These connect and relate to each other through a unifying force both known and unknown. The study of cause and effect, logic, and other sciences are attempts to discover the unifying factors behind creational actions. Actions and attributes are from one essence that we cannot describe, because description is dualistic and requires separation of subject and object, known and knower. All we know is that it is the source from which everything emanates.

The perceived physical boundaries are a by-product of sense perception, a manifestation of measurement. The products of perception are mental artefacts. Perception is invariably selective. Perception is selective according to value, attributing meaning according to need. The physical body-mind's need is survival. What drives evolution beyond mere survival of the body-mind is spiritual evolution, according to Gnostics which is the need for transcendence of the body-mind, the evolution or liberation of conditioned consciousness, from its own self-limiting activity toward its essential origin of pure soul consciousness.

Enlightenment aims at a fundamental correction of a wrong valuation of a separate fixed self. The perception of a self is a relative reality, a dualistic conditioned consciousness resulting from a limitation of perception and a value system that holds separation as the primary mode of knowledge. The sense of a separate self is physical, psychological and cultural.

Visual perception range is 1 micron in wavelength. If this is expanded to infinity, nothing would be seen as separate objects. Also the sense of a separate body would vanish. Sunlight has a finite bandwidth of electromagnetic energy, plus the visual receptors have a finite sensing range 0.4 to 0.7 microns. Infrared light is not seen but felt as heat. Ultraviolet light is not seen or felt but causes skin damage. If the apparatus of sense perception could register events at an extremely high rate, it would perceive only change, and no constancy, and would perceive no boundaries and no objects.

Recognition of separate objects and events is a psychological limitation that is related to context and valuation. The way we see the world as objects is a limitation of our sense perception system. The physical world is nothing but energy packets that form one big seamless energy source of varying intensities. We see and sense very selectively. We are biologically programmed to look and find what is of importance in a particular context. Biological evolution is concerned with survival. Humans have evolved the capability to transcend biological survival concerns. Our experience of the world is a result of sense perceptual selectivity and filtering. This is referred to as distortion or conditioning of consciousness. This shapes and influences the structure of the mind/brain, creating the state of conditioned consciousness. Conditioned consciousness is bound, whereas pure consciousness or awareness is free and unbound.

For lower organisms, conditioned consciousness is natural. It is necessary for survival. For humans, it is unnatural, because it causes suffering. The conditioned self sustains itself through a cycle of desire, grasping, possessing. And the mind ends up going deeper and deeper into a quagmire of sorrow, suffering, fear, conflict, desire and malice.

The Sufi, through creative expression, remembers and invokes the Divine order as it resides in a hidden state within all forms. To remember or invoke is to act in a form so that which is within may become known. The Sufi thus re-enacts the process of creation whereby the Divine came to know himself. Sufism begins with the way of knowledge, but carries it to its highest form: knowledge that illuminates. The way of illumination is often described as consisting of three attainments: the knowledge of certainty, the eye of certainty, and the truth of certainty.

Knowledge of certainty is gained from knowing the doctrine of the spiritual path. This forms the body or container of Sufism. The *eye of certainty* consists of the spiritual methods and practices contained within the body of Sufism, which lead to the *truth of certainty*: knowledge that illuminates.

Through an awakening to consciousness of the inner meaning of religious practices and rites, one becomes aware of that which is hidden, for the spirit or soul exists whether or not we are conscious of it. If we remain unaware, it remains passive and un-activated and only an allusion to the potentiality we contain.

The doctrine and method of Sufism are based on two concepts. These are the two testimonies of Islam: There is no God but Allah, and Mohammad is the Prophet of Allah. The first expresses the concept of Unity of Being, which annihilates all multiplicity and separation. It is to see the common denominator in all the multiplicities of form, to see the 'unity in multiplicity' of all creation, and to see that all circles have a centre regardless of size. The realisation of this concept annihilates multiplicity so that unity subsists.

The second testimony expresses the concept of the universal prototype human being. Through this concept one comes to see 'multiplicity in unity' to recognise the centre of the circle as unity containing all the multiplicities and accidents possible in the material world and to know that multiplicity subsists only because the unity within subsists.

The Sufi recognizes both the immanence and the transcendence of the Divine at one and the same time, and this is expressed in the doctrine. At the same time as the Divine is imminent, He is absolutely transcendent. At the same time as the Divine is 'nearer than the jugular vein', He is above every form, thought, or thing in the universe. There is a coincidence of opposites here that can be known only through the soul or Pure Consciousness, which discloses itself to the Sufi through spiritual intuition.

Sufism is not a rational philosophy. It is based on the nature of reality, which is transcendent. All purely philosophical systems are necessarily closed, because no mental form can encompass the infinite. Mental form itself is part of the infinite. It is only the spiritual heart, the instrument of intuition, that is above forms and capable of holding the throne of the Absolute. The goal of Sufism is to gather all multiplicity into unity, with the totality of one's being, in direct contemplation of spiritual realities, to come to know the qualitative unity that transcends the existence it unifies, at the same time as one integrates all aspects of self into a centre.

The journey begins with withdrawal from the material world in which one is drowned. To go from multiplicity in unity to

10 - The View of Self

unity in multiplicity, one must first die to the self, and, by dying, one is transformed, and then returns to the visible world. The ultimate meaning of the 'unity of being' is to 'see things as they really are' and to realise that all is reflected in the mirror of one's own being. It is the dissolution of the conditioned consciousness of the human being, who sees all things as independent and separate from the Divine, in order to realise that one was never separate from the Divine and the ultimate Absolute Truth: Allah in his Oneness is both immanent and transcendent.

The universe, in the Sufi view, is being re-created every moment. At every moment, what appears to be a time-connected universe returns to Allah. There is continuous, instantaneous expansion and contraction. The manifestation of actualised individual things occurs continually, as in successive waves. At every moment, creation is annihilated and re-created. With each heartbeat we die and are reborn. The world is in intense motion, ascending toward the vertical axis within all things to meet the descent of the Absolute in manifested forms. The flow occurs in such an orderly, successive manner, according to definite patterns, that we are unaware of it, and the world appears to us to stay the same. This ever-new creation is a process that only the human form endowed with self-consciousness can come to know.

Nay, they are in utter confusion regarding the new creation.
—*Qur'an 50.15*

It is the human self, a symbol of the feminine principle between the body and soul, that undertakes the quest and is transformed from its physical and sensible function into its psychic function and thence to its spiritual function. As the 'self' approaches the second transformation from sensible to spiritual, it becomes what the Sufi calls the *spiritual heart*, the instrument of intuition. It is the heart which finally unites with the Spirit. It is annihilated and experiences a spiritual death. It is then reborn, aligned with the soul, and attains subsistence. It knows that it exists through the Absolute and was never really separated from it.

Molecular Base

A single-cell organism has a membrane that is selectively permeable and separates the internal environment from the external environment. This is an example of an artifice that is necessary for self-preservation and self-replication. Our senses create the experience of a patchy world of separate objects. We are conditioned to see dense concentrations of energy that reflect visible light, and this light activates vision. We call these dense energy patches patterns 'matter'. The body is a dense patch of energy. The skin's surface is composed of negatively charged electron fields that repel any other surface with the same field. This produces the sense of touch and creates the experience of density and solidity.

The hierarchies of boundaries from subatomic particles and energy fields to biological cells and complex brains, are physical by-products, as well as the psychological by-products that lead to the conditioning of consciousness. Biological evolution is a process of evolution of changing boundaries employed by organisms in the struggle for survival. Human beings form the largest hierarchy of boundaries, creating the strongest conditioning and sense of self. The mind functions primarily within the parameters of this artificial reality that is biologically and culturally conditioned.

Human Drives

The spiritual seeker is driven by an evolutionary impulse from the core of his or her being, the heart. This hidden dynamic is termed the *soul*, the unconditioned essential reality within. Spiritual evolution transcends biological evolution, leading to a fundamental transformation of the individual both physically and psychologically. Evidence of this is recorded, from a few thousand years, in the scripture of authentic religions and wisdom traditions.

There is no ownership in truth. Ownership is a human convention, useful for conducting basic functional affairs. The sense of self is strengthened by claiming ownership of the body, thoughts, and states of mind. Liberation is bringing this cycle of imagined ownership to an end. Then life can be experienced directly without separation, fear, or lack. Each moment becomes an eternity. Our conditioning is deep and old. It requires relentless self-observation, knowledge, insight and practice to alter the deep-rooted patterns of desire and automatic responses of one's own mind and body.

Pure unbounded consciousness, like energy itself, is a universal phenomenon. When it is trapped within an individual brain, it becomes personal (conditioned consciousness). It identifies with the body-mind. Enlightenment is the liberation of consciousness from this identification. Pure soul consciousness is the underlying, ever-present reality. It continues to create the necessary impulse for conditioned consciousness to break free. Spiritual growth is a measure of the shifting of the point of balance toward realising the essential reality of soul consciousness.

Matter is a bounded island of energy made visible and distinct by the selectivity and limitations of the senses. We perceive the world as a collection of distinct material objects due to the way our senses work. Once the illusory world is created, our consciousness gets trapped in it and matter becomes our focus of interest. Most of our social, political, and economic institutions are built around control and manipulation of matter. Possession of objects is our criterion of wealth. Fighting over control of matter is our criterion of power. Because the material world is finite and relatively small, humans must compete fiercely to acquire ownership of objects. This is primitive animal psychology operating in the human context.

> *So long as I keep before me the ideal of an absolute observer of knowledge in the absence of any viewpoint, I can only see my situation as being a source of error. But once I have acknowledged that through it I am geared to all actions and all knowledge that are meaningful to me, then my contact with the social in the finitude of my situation is revealed to me as the starting point of all truth, including that of science*

and, since we have some idea of truth, since we are inside truth and cannot get outside it, all that I can do is define a truth within the situation.
—*Merleau-Ponty*

The entire existence is a transparent shimmering of the Divine, of primordial purity. But the Divine is not someplace else, it is just all of this shimmering of Pure Consciousness, referred to in Sufism as *Khayal*. It is self-existent and self-seen. It is nowhere else. It is the only constant in the entire Cosmos. It is the only reality in all of reality.

Revelation

In order to come to know the unity of being, the underlying undifferentiated consciousness, to realise the coincidence of its opposite aspects, transcendence and immanence, one needs a spiritual method. The method is derived from the second testimony that 'Muhammad is the Prophet of Allah'. The Prophet (PBUH) serves as the spiritual model by which one seeks to achieve the coincidence of opposites within the self. He serves as the place of gathering of all those universal and particular forms and meanings that are displayed throughout the universe.

The Prophet (PBUH) is an individual who, in form, manifests all the possibilities of humanity. By fully engaging in earthly life, he expresses his human nature. Through his receiving the revelation while in an unlettered or primordial state known as *fitra*, he is the receptacle of Divine nature. The Prophet is the universal prototype who unites the inward, eternal aspect of reality with the outward, phenomenal aspect. The Universal Prototype comprehends all individualities and unites all opposites in the infinite and universal nature of self. All Divine qualities are united and displayed. Hence the prototype becomes the means through which the supreme artisan or architect comes to display the splendour of creation.

The universal prototype or archetype symbolises four aspects of Divine manifestation. The archetype is the 'uncreated',

10 - The View of Self

pre-existent aspect within things. In the move toward creation it is the first articulation of the One, the first to contain objectivity. The archetype is also light: When the unmanifest darkness, ended and moved toward order, light came into being, of which wisdom is only a reflection. The archetype is also the active agent in the prototypical human form. It is the Divine's own image, the centre of the universe and the spirit of the Absolute. It is the word made manifest.

> *The Universal Prototype is the eye of the world, whereby the Absolute sees its own work.*
> —Ibn 'Arabi

COSMOLOGICAL SKETCH

The cosmos has two aspects. The first is expressed in the statement that the universe is not the Divine 'La ilaha'. The universe is relative, transient, changing, and therefore it is otherness, separateness, and a veil that separates us from the Divine. In its other aspect, the universe is none other than Allah, 'Illa Allah', because it is the universe that reveals the Divinity. Therefore the Cosmos both hides and reveals, veils and makes manifest. The Cosmos is both container, an expression of the unity of being, and contained, an expression of the universal prototype. The kaleidoscope of creation takes place from not-being to being, from 'desire' to 'be known'. The Divine conceives of the possibilities contained within, and then brings them forth. It is, in a sense, the Mystery as it steps out of the primordial darkness into light.

Because the Divine is infinite, knowledge of self is a part of its infiniteness. Being infinite and absolute, containing the totality of possibilities, it includes the possibility of negating the self and bringing the relative into being. Therefore the world exists because Allah is infinite, beyond any idea of limitation whatsoever.

The 'how' of creation is conceived as a triplicity. The One is perfect and beyond description. It is the principal and origin of all numbers. The first odd number therefore is not one, but three. Being 'with knowledge' necessarily implies three—knower, knowledge and known (a subject, a motion and an object).

Creation begins with the One at the point when it has singleness. This singleness has another three aspects that participate in the process of creation. First, there arises knowledge of self within the One as it moves toward manifestation. At this moment the archetypes or Divine names and qualities appear in Pure Consciousness. This marks the birth of multiplicity. Essence, the hidden treasure, moves to the level of the divinity. Subsequent to this, there arises the will, based on knowledge, to bring the archetypes from non-existence to phenomenal existence. On the basis of the Divine will, the Command 'Be!' is issued and the universe is created.

The triplicity of self-knowledge, will and command concerns the agent. This alone does not produce any effect. In order for the agent to be effective, there must be a recognition of the corresponding mode of triplicity on the part of the receiver, 'that which is to become known'. Creation can be actualised only when the two triplicities, active and passive, coincide.

The Divine in its unmanifest quality is above every quality we could ascribe to it. This is the Divine essence about which one can say nothing, for any description would only serve to limit or bind It. The Divine essence manifests Itself, however, in the direction of creation through stages, the first of which is the archetypes, the possibilities of which are contained within the absolute.

Divine emanation is a twofold process: intelligible and sensible. The emanation brings the archetypes into intelligible existence. Known as the Divine names and qualities or attributes, these archetypes are the possibilities contained within the Absolute. They occupy a middle position between the Absolute and the sensible world. They are passive in relation to the Absolute, and at the same time they are active in relation to the worlds below them. They are actualised in the sensible phenomenal world according to the preparedness of the particular sensible form that they take on. It is through such archetypes as the names of Allah that one invokes or calls upon the Absolute, to transform one's own self. As the names are the hierarchies of being between

10 - The View of Self

us and the Absolute, they serve as a bridge between us and the Divine Essence.

The Divine Names are often classified as names of essence, of actions and of qualities. Names of essence, such as *Ahad* (the One) *Haqq* (the Truth or Absolute), and *Nur* (Light), concern the divinity and would exist whether or not there had been creation. They are aspects completely independent of us. Names of Actions, such as *Khaliq* (Creator) relate to creation. Names of qualities include *Karim* (Generous), *Hayy* (Living) and *Shakur* (Thankful). The names are also classified as names of majesty, *Jalal*, and names of beauty, *Jamal*. The Sufi invokes Allah through the names of beauty, because they symbolize ascent toward the Essence, whereas the names of majesty refer to the descent of creation.

This first stage of emanation is conceived of as the One, *Ahadiyyah*, moving toward Oneness, *Wahidiyyah*. The archetypes are noumena, forms that are outwardly and actually intelligible, but inwardly and potentially sensible.

The second stage of emanation occurs when the shadows of the archetypes read the world of symbols, *A'lam al-mithal/Malakut*, and the shadows of the world of symbols reach the phenomenal world, *Mulk*. The phenomenal world is the manifestation of these higher worlds and reflects the splendour of multiplicity. The phenomenon is a form that is outwardly and actually sensible. It can be grasped by the five outer senses of sight, hearing, smell, taste and touch. Outward forms act as sensible containers for the archetypes, which are in turn intelligible containers for aspects of the Absolute.

The transitional world of symbols is that by virtue of which sensible measurable forms correspond exactly to unmeasurable intellections. That is, 'I' can mentally comprehend an idea without a form, but 'I' can actualise my own transformation only by the practice of rites in the presence of symbolic forms. The universe is often referred to as the shadow of the Absolute: something that has relative existence by virtue of being a sensible determination of an undetermined archetype.

Reflective Mystery

The relation between a shadow and that which casts it is like the relation of the phenomenon to the cause of its noumenon. In order to have a shadow, one must have three things:

1. first, something that will cast a shadow;
2. second, a place where the shadow may fall; and
3. third, light by which the shadow is made known.

In Sufi terminology, it is the Absolute in the relative aspect of self that casts the shadow. The place is the world of archetypes: the place of the essences of possible things. If there were no place, the shadow would remain intelligible only, like a seed in a tree. The light by which the shadow is made known is a manifestation of the Absolute as well. Shining on the world of archetypes, it casts a shadow on the lower world of symbols which finally reach the phenomenal world. If the upper world did not veil the light, and cast a shadow that is all that we see, the light would be blinding.

> *Non-being is a mirror, the world an image, and man Is the eye of the image, in which the person is hidden. Thou art the eye of the image, and He the light of the eye.*
> *Who has ever seen the eye through which all things are seen?*
> *The world has become a man, and man a world.*
> *There is no clearer explanation than this.*
> *When you look well into the root of the matter,*
> *He is at once seen, seeing eye, and thing seen.*
> *The holy tradition had declared this,*
> *And 'without eye or ear' demonstrated it.*
> —Mahmud Shabistari

The preparedness within a thing, its inner archetype, is actualised in an intelligible form at the moment when its name flows into it through a word. The Divine Spirit flows into a thing through the process of the Divine breath, the breath of the

10 - The View of Self

Divine name *Rahman* (Compassionate). The Compassionate is the highest of the names. When there is a desire to be known, and the preparedness arises within a thing, the Divine as compassion extends itself as archetype to the thing and becomes its receptivity and its ability to receive theophany.

The receptivity is actually what the archetype, in its essence, desires. Compassion is given without any discrimination. *Rahim* (Merciful) is the complement and is given only for an act done.

Compassion in a sense is the universal form of Divine giving. Mercy is the particular aspect. Through the name of Compassion, the absolute breathes out upon the other names. This breathing out is a means of bringing things into existence. By means of the command 'Be!' the Absolute, through Compassion, sends into the external phenomenal world that which has been latent within its Essence.

The Divine breath, *Ruh*, is essentially nature itself. Just as the breath contains all the forms of the universe in a potential state and actualises them by exhaling, so nature holds all forms of expression in a potential state of preparedness in which they await the appearance of the breath of the Compassionate, the spirit, in order to be known. This breath is essentially the initial act of the metaphysic of Love. Love is the cause and secret of all creation and thereby the principle of all motion, from desire to being known. The creation of the world was the motion of Love toward perfection and completion. The absolute Loves to be perfect in both types of forms: intelligible and sensible.

ORIGINS

The self has its origin in the spiritual world. When it is attached to the body, it descends from the world of light to this world of darkness, dark because of its symbolic distance from the light source. If the body with its limited desires proves the stronger, the self becomes heavier, more materially oriented, dense and opaque. If, however, the self becomes aware of its captivity and conscious of its imprisonment within the body, then, and only then, can the journey begin.

Thus, the moment of consciousness is awareness of the exile, the moment when the self realises the illusion of this life and yearns to return to its origin where it was one with the light of unity. Only then does the 'self' discover where it is, where it came from, and where it is to go. The human self contains the possibility of uniting the opposites within by means of its own consciousness. The self, the feminine principle of the reflective Moon within, is united with the soul, the masculine principle of the Sun within. Then the desire that sought knowledge becomes known. The way of the Sufi is to become aware of the possibilities that exist within the human self, to conceive them, and then, through spiritual practice, to actualise them.

In the Self's earthly journey, having come from the non-physical world, it must first of all become less subtle and more dense. In this evolving process, it becomes the vegetative self, allowing the form within the womb to have the same function of feeding and growth as from plants: the ability to transform foreign substances into its own form. As the form grows in the womb, it develops the animal self, in which it acquires the ability of motion. At birth, the animal self is completed, as the form exhibits various desires. However, not until adolescence does the self pass from potential consciousness to being able to actualise the Adamic consciousness with the appearance of the rational self. The quest may begin now. The ability to transform the self has come into existence.

> *I died as a mineral and became a plant, I died as plant and rose to animal, I died as animal and I was Man. Why should I fear? When was I less by dying?*
> *Yet once more I shall die as Man, to soar with angels blest; but even from angelhood*
> *I must pass on: all except God doth perish.*
> *When I have sacrificed my angel-soul, I shall become what no mind ever conceived.*
> *Oh, let me not exist! for non-existence proclaims in organ tones, 'To Him we shall return'.*
> — *Rumi*

10 - The View of Self

The first stage of the journey is to retrace one's steps, to return to one's primordial nature, *fitra*: to become a form without desires. That is, one actively denies self-desires, and exists with the faculties of feeding, growth, and motion. It is a return to complete potentiality before any masks were assumed. To be awakened is to cross the bridge to one's primordial nature and then enter through the gateway, *mihrab*.

Once inside the gateway, the self encounters the five senses, that is, the physical instruments of the sensory structure. Whereas the first stage consists of denial, the second is saturation. This is perhaps the most treacherous part of the journey, for one is often waylaid by the sensory pleasures and detained from journeying further. Desires of the carnal or commanding self reappear as the dragon, and one must fight one's way forward.

The psychic aspect of the feminine principle consists of the five internal senses: common sense: *hiss mushtarak*; imaginal: *khayal*; valuation: *wahm*; memory: *thakira*; and intellect: *mufakira*. The functions of these internal senses are described according to form and meaning. Common sense is the ability to integrate phenomena into meanings. The imaginal is the ability to preserve forms, valuation is the ability of ascribing values to forms, and memory is the ability to preserve forms and meanings. The intellect or reflection is the intuitive ability to govern both sensible phenomena and intelligible noumena so that a balance is always preserved. The intellect is the spiritual heart. This function contains both the feminine principle, as manifested in the sensible, and the masculine principle, as manifested in the intelligible. Its role is to activate and join the two.

Thus the inner senses are just one part of a larger totality of the feminine principle of the self, incorporating the outer senses, which is on the quest toward spiritual becoming and union. It is during this phase of the journey that one meets with the psychic forces within: *jinn*. They constantly intrude with temptations and inclinations that one must actively put aside, or once again one will be hindered from continuing the journey.

STAGES

The Self, once awakened, goes through three spiritual stages. The first stage is the awakening to consciousness of the existence of the commanding self: *nafs ammarah*. At the second stage, the feminine principles come into play, and this is called the blaming self: *nafs lawwamah*, the self's awareness of its own imperfections. Here the struggle between good and evil is enacted. Finally, the self reaches the spiritual stage of peace, *nafs mutma'inah*, when it is reintegrated with the soul, and at rest in certainty.

> O Soul at peace, return unto thy Lord, well-pleased, well-pleasing. Enter thou among my servants. Enter thou my paradise.
> —Qur'an 39.29

The Islamic model of the hierarchy of being, differentiates between seven levels or layers:

1. Transcendent Unity, *al-ahadiyya:* the state of non-determination, being the Absoluteness and pure Essence, not meaning that the limits of absoluteness and negation are affirmative in this state, but that being in this state transcends the addition of qualities and attributes, and is too sacred to be defined by any limit, even the limit of absoluteness. It is the state of the ineffable Essence that refuses human understanding. It is the state of non-qualified and non-determined existence that lies beyond human conception. As such, it cannot be the object of any distinctive knowledge, and is therefore inaccessible to the human mind.

2. Divine Solitude, *al-wahda:* the state of first determination that represents Allah's knowledge of his Essence, attributes, and all existents in their non-differentiated, indistinctive mode of being. Ontologically, it mediates between transcendent unity and divine uniqueness and is also referred to as the state of the Muhammadan Reality.

10 - The View of Self

3. Divine Uniqueness, *al-wahdaniyya*: the state of second determination that represents God's knowledge of his Essence, attributes, and all existents in their differentiated, distinctive mode of being. It is also referred to as the state of Adamic reality. The first three states of being concern being in the primordial stage, yet primordiality as well as precedency and succession in the above states must be understood as intellectual levels of consciousness and not temporal qualifications.

4. The World of Spirits, *'alam al-arwah*: the state of simple, abstract cosmic entities or archetypes, those in the likeness of which, and in accordance with whose essences, manifestation is fashioned.

5. The World of Similitude, *'alam al-mithal*: the state of subtle, composed cosmic entities, those that are not susceptible to division, portioning, separation, or conjunction.

6. The World of Bodies, *'alam al-ajsam*: the state of dense, composed cosmic entities, those that are susceptible to division, portioning, separation, and conjunction.

7. Human, *al-insan*: the last and the sum total of all manifest states, the bodily and the spiritual as well as the states of Divine uniqueness and Divine solitude.

The human form is the place of gathering of dualities, both inner and outer. The inner duality exists within the form and is essentially the vision one has of oneself. The outer duality exists between forms; it is the vision one has of oneself as reflected in another form. In the inner duality, men and women are the same. The meaning of the form does not differ. The masculine and feminine principles of soul and self exist in both, irrespective of outer forms. The outer duality consists of the physical forms of man and woman. Thus it is only through the inner form that the gathering of opposites may be accomplished.

The process whereby the self enters the quest lies in the techniques and methods of Sufism, which are centred upon the ability one has to focus. The object of focus becomes the Divine so that we become Divine-centred. One's urges are stronger toward outwardness, and thus all methods of Sufism seek the centre. Without the ability to meditate or contemplate, it is impossible to control the urges of the self. You must seek certain stillness. You cannot hear the voice of the Divine until you are still. The method is one of spiritual alchemy. Through transformation, the substance of the self is changed.

Everything in creation is a symbol for everything perceived by the outer senses and may be conceived through the inner senses as a sign of a higher state of reality. It is through the use of symbols that one is awakened, it is through symbols that one is transformed, and it is through symbols that one expresses. Symbols are realities contained within the nature of things. The entire journey in the Divine is a journey in symbols, in which one is constantly aware of the higher reality within things. Symbols reflect both Divine transcendence and Divine immanence. They refer to both the universal aspect of creation and the particular aspect of tradition.

> *Hast thou not seen how Allah citeth a symbol?*
> *A good word is a good tree*
> *Its root set firm,*
> *And its branches in heaven;*
> *Giving its fruit at every season,*
> *By the leave of its Lord.*
> *So God citeth symbols for men*
> *That they may remember.*
> —Qur'an 14.29-31

10 - The View of Self

We must be still and still moving; Into another intensity; For a further union, a deeper communion; Through the dark cold and the empty desolation, The wave cry, the wind cry, the vast waters; Of the petrel and the porpoise. In my end is my beginning.
—*T. S. Eliot*

There is neither good nor bad qualities in the Self. The Self is free from all qualities. Qualities pertain to the mind only. It is beyond quality. If there is unity, there will also be duality. The numerical one gives rise to other numbers. The truth is neither one nor two. It is as it is.
—*Ramana Maharshi*

CURRENT VIEW

The German philosopher Thomas Metzinger, in his brilliant book *The Ego Tunnel*, attempts to convince us, through studying the phenomena of the phantom limb and his own out-of-body experiences, that there is no such thing as the self. He asserts that it has now become clear that we will never solve the philosophical puzzle of consciousness, that is, how it can arise in the brain, which is a purely physical object—if we don't come to terms with this simple proposition: that to the best of our current knowledge there is nothing, no indivisible entity, that is us, neither in the brain nor in some metaphysical realm beyond this world. So when we speak of conscious experience as a subjective phenomenon, what is the entity having these experiences?

What is experienced in the case of the phantom limb phenomena is what he calls the content of the phenomenal self-model (PSM)—the conscious model of the organism as a whole that is activated by the brain. ("Phenomenal" is used here, and throughout, in the philosophical sense, as pertaining to what is known purely experientially, through the way in which things subjectively appear to you.) The content of the PSM is the Ego.

The PSM of homosapiens is probably one of nature's best inventions. It is an efficient way to allow a biological organism to consciously conceive of itself (and others) as a whole. Thus it enables the organism to interact with its internal world as well as with the external environment in an intelligent and holistic manner. Most animals are conscious to one degree or another, but their PSMs are not the same as ours. Our evolved type of conscious self-model is unique to the human brain, in that by representing the process of representation itself, we can catch ourselves in the act of knowing. We mentally represent ourselves as representational systems, in phenomenological real-time. This ability turned us into thinkers of thoughts and readers of minds, and it allowed biological evolution to explode into cultural evolution.

Conscious experience is like a tunnel. Modern neuroscience has demonstrated that the content of our conscious experience is not only an internal construct but also an extremely selective way of representing information. This is why it is a tunnel: What we see and hear, or what we feel and smell and taste, is only a small fraction of what actually exists out there. Our conscious model of reality is a low dimensional projection of the inconceivably richer physical reality surrounding and sustaining us. Our sensory organs are limited. They evolved for reasons of survival, not for depicting the enormous wealth and richness of reality in all its unfathomable depth. Therefore, the ongoing process of conscious experience is not so much an image of reality as a tunnel through reality.

Whenever our brains successfully pursue the ingenious strategy of creating a unified and dynamic inner portrait of reality, we become conscious. First, our brains generate a world-simulation so perfect that we do not recognise it as an image in our minds. Then, they generate an inner image of ourselves as a whole. This image includes not only our bodies and our psychological states but also our relationship to the past and the future, as well as to other conscious beings. The internal image of the person-as-a-whole is the phenomenal Ego, the 'I' or 'self' as it appears in conscious experience. By placing the self-model within the world-model, a centre is created. That centre is what we experience as ourselves: the Ego. It is the origin of what philosophers

10 - The View of Self

often call the first-person perspective. We are not in direct contact with outside reality or with ourselves, but we do have an inner perspective. We can use the word 'I.' We live our conscious lives in the Ego Tunnel.

In ordinary states of consciousness, there is always someone having the experience—someone consciously experiencing him or herself as directed toward the world, as a self in the act of attending, knowing, desiring, willing and acting. There are two major reasons for this. First, we possess an integrated inner image of ourselves that is firmly anchored in our feelings and bodily sensations; the world-simulation created by our brains includes the experience of a point of view. Second, we are unable to experience and introspectively recognise our 'self-models' as models; much of the self-model is, as philosophers might say, transparent.

Transparency simply means that we are unaware of the medium through which information reaches us. The central claim of this book and the theory behind it, the self-model theory of subjectivity is that the conscious experience of being a self emerges because a large part of the PSM in your brain is transparent. The Ego, as noted, is simply the content of your PSM at this moment (your bodily sensations, emotional state, perceptions, memories, acts of will, thoughts). But it can become the Ego only because you are constitutionally unable to realise that all of this is just the content of a simulation in your brain.

The Ego and the Tunnel are evolved representational phenomena, a result of dynamical self-organisation on many levels. Ultimately, subjective experience is a biological data format, a highly specific mode of presenting information about the world by letting it appear as if it were an Ego's knowledge. But no such things as 'selves' exist in the world. A biological organism, as such, is not a self. An Ego is not a self either but merely a form of representational content—namely, the content of a transparent self-model activated in the organism's brain.

The idea of an Ego Tunnel is based on an older notion that has been around for quite some time now. It is the concept of a 'reality tunnel'. The general idea is this: Yes, there is an outside world, and, yes, there is an objective reality, but in moving through this world, we constantly apply unconscious filter mechanisms, and in doing so, we unknowingly construct our own individual world, which is our 'reality tunnel.' We are never directly in touch with reality as such, because these filters prevent us from seeing the world as it is. The filtering mechanisms are our sensory systems and our brains, the architecture of which we inherited from our biological ancestors, as well as our prior beliefs and implicit assumptions. The construction process is largely invisible. In the end, we see only what our reality tunnel allow us to see, and most of us are completely unaware of this fact. We do not create an individual world but only a world-model. Moreover, the whole idea of potentially being directly in touch with reality is a sort of romantic folklore. We know the world only by using representations, because (correctly) representing something is what knowing is.

Conscious experience, as such, is an internal affair. Whatever else may or may not be true about consciousness, once all the internal properties of your nervous system are set, all the properties of your conscious experience—its subjective content and the way it feels to you—are fully determined. By 'internal' I mean not only spatial but also temporal internality - whatever is taking place right now, at this very moment. As soon as certain properties of your brain are fixed, everything you are experiencing at this very moment is also fixed. While we are drinking in all the colors, sounds, and smells—the diverse range of our emotions and sensory perceptions—it's hard to believe that all of this is merely an internal shadow of something inconceivably richer. But it is. Shadows do not have an independent existence.

> *Why are you unhappy? Because 99.9 per cent of everything you think, and of everything you do, is for yourself, and there isn't one.*
> *—Wei Wu Wei*

> *Spiritual awakening is about discovering what's true. Anything that's not about getting to the truth must be discarded. Truth isn't about knowing things—you already know too much. It's about un knowing. It's not about becoming true, it's*

10 - The View of Self

about un becoming false so that all that's left is truth. If you want to become a priest or a lama or a rabbi or a theologian, then there's a lot to learn—tons and tons. But if you want to figure out what's true, then it's a whole different process and the last thing you need is more knowledge.
—Jed McKenna

11 - The View of the Imaginal

He said: Nay! cast down. then lo! their cords and their rods, it was imaged to him on account of their sorcery as if they were moving.
—Qur'an 20.66

In this night journey I gained the meanings of all the Divine names. I saw that they all go back to a single Named Object and a Single Entity. That Named Object was what I was witnessing, and that Entity was my own existence. So my journey had been only in myself. I provided no indications of any but myself. It was from here that I came to know that I am a sheer servant and that there is nothing whatsoever of lordship within me.
—Ibn 'Arabi

At the highest levels of self-realization, knowledge of self, yields the recognition that there is nothing in existence but the self, because nothing can be found in the entire universe but God's self-disclosure. At its most comprehensive and unified, that Divine self-disclosure is simply the form in which human beings were created. One who realizes this station recognizes his absolute subservience to the Real and acts as God's servant in all that he does. Achieving this station can only come through 'gnosis,' that is, through self-recognition. Ibn 'Arabi advises the seeker, 'Do not hope to recognize yourself through other than yourself, for there is no other'.
—Ibn 'Arabi

Mundus Imaginalis

The great Sufi Shaykh Ibn 'Arabi is considered the expounder par excellence of the Sufi path of knowledge. His philosophy of imagination is a journey in consciousness, traversing the hierarchy of existence toward its principle in the Divine. Imagination had long been discussed by Muslim philosophers to highlight the intermediacy of the subjective realm, which is an image of both the knowing self and the known object. This subjective realm came into being when Allah blew His spirit into Adam's clay. It is none other than the soul, which arises at the meeting point of light and darkness, awareness and unawareness. Philosophers considered the imaginal as one of several internal faculties or senses. Ibn 'Arabi universalised the concept, showing that it properly designates everything other than God. All things are images of being consciousness, and all things are also images of utter nothingness. All things shimmer between being and non-being. Each is an interspace, *barzakh*, between other things, spatially and temporally.

Human beings, made in Allah's image, have a unique relationship with both Allah and the cosmos. This gives them the ability to grasp, understand, and realise him in both his distance and his nearness. Ibn 'Arab calls the faculty of understanding Allah as distant 'reason' *'aql*, and the faculty of seeing Allah as near 'imagination' *khayal*.

If the heart, the unitary intellectual centre at the root of the human selfhood, is to perceive the word of Allah resounding in itself, it must open what Ibn 'Arab calls its 'two eyes', the eye of reason and the eye of imagination, or discursive thought and mythic vision. Only the fully realised heart can grasp the symbolic significance of revelation, because neither reason nor imagination on its own can see the fullness of the realities, rights and responsibilities established by the Absolute *Haqq*.

The eye of reason is the characteristic tool of the theologians and jurists. It is inadequate because it can only see Allah as transcendent. It recognises that Allah cannot be known in Himself, so it describes Him as totally apart from every created thing and

11 - The View of the Imaginal

every quality. Left to its own devices, discursive reason will eventually misunderstand and distort the messages of the prophets, which are primarily anthropomorphic and mythic, and refuse to acknowledge that anything positive can be said about Allah. Excessive stress on rational thought pushes the Divine into total transcendence. When this process is not kept in balance with the eye of myth and imagination, rational analysis eventually results in a scientific rationality, completely oblivious to the relationship between Allah, the world, and the human soul. Excessive dependence on reason leads to agnosticism and atheism, because it declares that Allah is absolutely unknowable and therefore any relationship cannot be established, including revelation.

The eye of imagination sees Allah as immanent. It recognises Allah's signs and marks in all things. It perceives the universe as the expression of Divine intelligence. It finds Allah's names and attributes manifest everywhere in the world and the self, and it describes Allah in the positive terms supplied by revelation and the natural realm. The eye of imagination thrives on myth and symbol, and it sees things not simply as signs and pointers to Allah, but as the actual presence of the *Haqq*.

Left to its own devices, however, it will divinise the world and its productions and fall into the assertion of many gods. *True knowledge or realisation* is not possible unless one sees with both eyes, recognising Allah in both His transcendence and His immanence, both His absoluteness and His infinity. When we fail to see the Divine face wherever we look, we fall either into the one-sided transcendentalism that is characteristic of religious fundamentalism or the atheism and agnosticism that are characteristic of secular and scientific fundamentalism.

> *To Allah belong the East and the West; whithersoever you turn, there is the Face of Allah; Allah is All-embracing, All-knowing.*
> —*Quran 2.115*

'Know that you are an imagination', Ibn 'Arabi says, 'and everything that you perceive, and of which you would say, "this is not me", is also an imagination. So the whole being is an imagination within an imagination'. Here Ibn 'Arabi alludes to more than one level of imagination. In keeping with his universal hierarchy and concept of 'shadow' Ibn 'Arabi distinguishes three ontologically different levels of imagination: a transcendental, unrestricted imagination, *khayal mutlaq*, or absolute imagination; an all-encompassing imagination, *khayal munfasil*, detached imagination; and an encompassed imagination, *khayal muttasil*, attached imagination.

The notion of imagination, however, still designates two different, yet related, things: a state of being and a creative capacity. As a creative capacity, the 'detached' and 'attached' polarity differentiates between the Divine and human modes of creativity. Attached imagination, Ibn 'Arabi explains, designates our ability to abstract, conceive of, and manipulate forms. It is our imagining faculty operating within the human psychological framework. It is called 'attached' because it is an imagination conjoined to the imagining subject and inseparable from Him, and it is a 'dependent imagination' because it depends, in its existence, on 'detached imagination', that He is 'autonomous'. 'Detached' or 'autonomous imagination', by contrast, refers to a higher creative capacity that causes all imaginable forms to exist. The forms conceived by 'attached imagination' are extracted by the senses from natural forms, which are a part of the cosmic forms that belong to a self-subsisting presence independent of the imagining subject.

Detached imagination is Divine imagination, Allah imagining the world. It is the presence of the world in the Divine mind. Attached imagination is human imagination, man imagining the forms of existents brought into existence by the creative power of Divine imagination. It is the presence of things in human consciousness.

Attached imagination depends upon detached imagination, and the human act of imagining is no more than a participation in the latter. Ibn 'Arabi says that from this detached imagination the attached imagination derives. Although both have creative power, detached and attached imaginations are fundamentally

11 - The View of the Imaginal

different: one is permanent and the other is transitory. The permanence of the detached derives from Divine eternity, whereas the transience of the attached is a reflection of the human's temporality. The distinction between attached and detached imagination is that the attached vanishes when the one who is imagining vanishes; the detached is an essential presence permanently receiving meanings and spirits so that it embodies them by its special capacity.

Human imagination has the power of participating in the world of detached imagination and it is capable of composing an infinite number of different kinds of images. But in that, it is confined to the sensible domain and its elementary data are therefore limited. It follows that out of the limited data that human imagination has at its disposal, humans have the capacity to synthesize as many forms as there are possibilities latent in the world of detached imagination.

As an all-encompassing, permanent presence, the world of detached imagination can then be seen as governing the human attached imagination by setting an immutable code or natural patterned structure for it. Such a code, whose content is made up of the cosmic realities, is necessary to prevent the human imagination from degenerating into fantasy.

When participating in this realm of realities, the world we live in, human imagination can become either a valuable source of knowledge when it complies with the realities of that code or a corrupt fantasy when it does not. The code differentiates the true forms of consciousness that we experience as outer reality, and our fantasies about reality.

DIVINE PATTERNING

For Sufis, combinations of the Divine names constitute the regulating patterns of existence, varying according to the subjects they designate. The creation of the world, for example, requires a pattern different from that required for the subsistence of the world after it has been created. Likewise, different modalities of the Divine names reveal different patterns. A different combination of attributes is needed to know Allah the creator of the world than the one needed to know him as the self-sufficient. Sufis discern a structure in these infinite varieties of patterns, based on a perceived hierarchy in both single and combined Divine names. Quadrature and triplicity occupy, with regard to the creative process, primary positions in this hierarchy.

Sufis consider that Allah's manifestation and becoming knowable coincides with the creation of the world. For this creative emergence to be fulfiled, a certain combination of Divine names is necessary. According to Ibn 'Arabi, this is achieved through four principal names: the Living, *al-hayy;* the Knowing, *al-'alim;* the Willing, *al-murid;* and the Powerful, *al-qadir*, which manifest the attributes of Life, Knowledge, Will and Power.

> *The power of my imagination took me to the point where my love embodied my Beloved before my eyes in the outside world, just as Gabriel used to embody himself to the Messenger of God. I could not bear to gaze upon Him, yet He addressed me and I listened to Him and understood what He said. For several days He left me in a state where I could not eat.*
> —Ibn 'Arabi

Finding the Unseen

Ibn 'Arabi's first topic is always the true reality itself, which is the Divine. His second topic is the cosmos, which is defined as everything other than the Divine. When employing the technical language of philosophy and theology, he typically calls the Divine *wujud*, a word that is usually translated as 'being' or 'existence'. In our context it is synonymous with Pure Consciousness.

Consciousness, or *wujud*, is not simply the fact of being or existing—the fact that something is there to be found as some sort of cold inanimateness within which life and joy and love are cosmic accidents. An implicit if not explicit side to the use of this term is that the Divine's own life, awareness, and consciousness course through everything that exists, although His attributes display themselves most clearly in what we call 'living

11 - The View of the Imaginal

things' plants, animals and human beings.

Wujud is the reality of finding, which is to say that it is awareness, consciousness, understanding and knowledge. As a technical term, it was used to designate 'finding God,' that is, coming to direct awareness and consciousness of the Divine Reality. It was practically a synonym of words like *witnessing* and *unveiling*, which also play prominent roles in Ibn 'Arabi's writings. Consciousness designates not only the incomparable and ineffable reality of the Divine, but also the immanent presence of the Divine in the knower's awareness. The Gnostics look with both eyes, and they perceive being as both absent, because it is none other than the Divine Essence, and present, because it is none other than the absolute self-disclosure as the selfhood of the knower.

In Ibn 'Arabi's terminology, consciousness means not only being and existence, the objective dimension of reality, but also finding and awareness, the subjective dimension of reality. Islamic philosopher Seyyed Hossein Nasr noted that the three Arabic words *wujud, wijdan, wajd*, 'being–consciousness–ecstasy,' are all derived from the same root *wjd*, and that each word stresses a different implication of Ultimate Reality.

In itself, absolute being is the non-manifest, the hidden treasure. However, it loved to be known, so it created the universe in order to be known. Those who recognise and realise the truth of existence are true human beings. But people cannot know and recognise the Divine unless it makes itself known to them, and it does so by revealing itself in three basic modes: the universe, the human self, and scripture. Scripture is the key that opens the door to the universe and the self. Self-expressive consciousness employs scripture to stir up human understanding. Without recourse to it, people will not be able to fathom themselves and the cosmos. If they do not come to know and recognize themselves, they will not know their origin. The essence cannot be known in itself, but it can be known inasmuch as it discloses itself in the form of its most beautiful names.

From the Sufi perspective, the virtues that people must acquire are precisely the Divine names and attributes, for it is these that are latent in the human soul. Life in this world is a process through which the traces and properties of the Divine names come to be actualised. Revelation is necessary if people are to become qualified by the names in proper harmony and equilibrium. Humans need Divine guidance if they are to actualize the traits of the names as virtues and to avoid their deformation as vices. If people display the traces of Divine attributes such as severity and wrath and fail to keep them properly confined through justice, compassion, and generosity, they will be dominated by cruelty and arrogance. Ibn 'Arabi refers to the assumption of the traits of the Divine names as the very definition of the spiritual life: 'Assuming the character traits of Allah, that is Sufism'.

The existent entities of the universe are the infinite differentiations and delimitations to which the radiance of real existence is susceptible. Each creature is a self-disclosure of consciousness, but it does not truly exist, because consciousness alone is truth. It follows that each creature is Being/not Being, He/not He, Allah/not Allah.

In himself the Divine will never be found. And only the Divine who will never be found is truly the infinite Divine who is no different from true reality. If the Divine in Himself cannot be sought, what are the seekers seeking? What have the Sufis been singing about in their poetry if not love for truth? Ibn 'Arabi replies that they are not seeking the Divine essence, but only inasmuch as they understand and embrace Him, that is, the Divine as He shows Himself to them. This entity that discloses itself to them, however, is not the absolute essence. It is the radiance and manifestation of the absolute, not the absolute itself.

THE STATION OF NO STATION

Ibn 'Arabi calls human perfection 'the station of no station'. Everyone other than the archetypal human being stands in a specific station delimited and defined by the objects of his aspiration. The archetype alone stands in no station, because he alone has fully actualised a love that has no specific object. Rather, the object of his love is the infinite Divine essence, which remains forever inaccessible. The archetype is defined by his lack of definition. He loves the 'nothing' that is the source of everything. He has perfected the Divine form, for he is indefinable and unrestricted, just like the object of his love. By living in no thing and no station, he is free of all things and all stations. By being poor and needy toward all things, he is poor and needy toward nothing, which is to say that he is poor and needy only toward the Divine and wealthy and independent only through him.

For Ibn 'Arabi, time and place relations, in contrast with entities, which are real things that are not necessarily manifest things. Time and place designate interrelationships among things, but they themselves are not things. There is nothing out there that can properly be called time or place. From Ibn 'Arabi's standpoint, if we want to verify the real, objective world and come up with a valid theory of how things hold together, we need to go beyond appearances and surface relationships. We need to penetrate into the principles and essences. Time and space are abstract concepts and insubstantial relationships, that is, simply how things appear to us.

Space therefore designates the location of something in the visible world, so the concept involves a certain fixity. But things are not in fact fixed, because both their being and their location change. As soon as we perceive change, time enters the picture. Time designates change and movement in the realm of being. It refers to changing relationships in the appearance of the cosmos in consciousness. The cosmos can never be fixed and stable, because permanence and stability are attributes of the absolute, not creation. Time is a name that we give to the pattern of ongoing changes that occur in the face of the cosmos or consciousness. Both time and place are demanded by the realm generation and corruption. Generation means coming to be as a result of the Divine's creative act, and corruption means disappearance. To speak of manifestation is to speak of place, because it is localised. To speak of corruption is to speak of change, and changes are described in terms of time.

Eternity and Time

The relationship between eternity and time is the relationship between the absolute and the world, a fixed relationship of eternity or a changing relationship of time. The Qur'an mentions 'the Days of Allah', and Ibn 'Arabi takes this as a reference to the prefiguration of temporal differentiation in the Divine knowledge. It is the Days of Allah that give birth to the unfolding temporal cycles of our world.

Allah has days of differing length that are related to various names. The Qur'an says that the angels and the Spirit rise up to Allah in a day whose length is 50,000 of our years, and it relates this 50,000-year day to the Divine name *dhu'lma'arij*, the 'Possessor of the Ladders'. The Qur'an also speaks of a 1,000-year day, and Ibn 'Arabi explains that it is connected to the name 'Lord': *rabb*. He also mentions several other Divine days of varying length, each related to a specific Divine name. The most all-embracing of the days of Allah is the 'day of the essence', to which Ibn 'Arabi finds a reference in the verse, 'Each day He is upon some task'. God's Essence, denoted here by the pronoun He, is absolute, unchanging. It may seem that the Day of the Essence is the longest of the Divine days. This is true: however, Ibn 'Arabi points out that from our standpoint, it is the shortest.

Its length is one instant, which is the present moment. There is no time shorter than the present moment, which is defined precisely as the instant that cannot be divided into parts. But, this shortest of Divine days lasts forever. We never leave the present moment, because we never leave the Divine presence.

To be an image is to be an interspace between an object that casts the image and the locus in which the image appears. It is located in a no-land between being and non-existence, light and darkness, consciousness and unawareness. As the very stuff of the soul, imagination marks the point where the active vitality of intelligence encounters the signs perceived by the senses. Invisible realities come down into imagination embodied as notions and dreams, and the objects of sense perception rise up to

11 - The View of the Imaginal

imagination and become the landscape of the soul. Awareness and unawareness, depth and surface, meaning and words, spirit and clay, inward and outward, non-manifest and manifest—all coalesce and become one.

As two all-comprehensive images of the Absolute, cosmos and soul reflect each other. The universe is outward, deployed, dispersed and objectified; the soul inward, concentrated, focused and subjectified. The soul is aware and conscious the world unaware and unknowing. Through its inwardness, the soul finds itself and others, and through its outwardness, the world discloses what is potentially knowable to the soul.

Allah taught Adam all the names; everything deployed and dispersed in the universe is already known to the primordial soul. Regaining Adamic perfection means to remember who we are and to recognise what we know. 'All the names' means every possibility of being and becoming present in the soul, every word articulated in the All-merciful Breath, the *Ruh*. The qualities and characteristics of created things are in fact the names of their Creator. Following the path of realisation, the soul comes to experience the designations of the names in its own imaginal realm, where being and awareness are one.

BEWILDERMENT

All human knowledge is the articulation of consciousness. Everything we know is our self, because awareness and knowledge are situated inside the self, not outside it. What we know is the image of what lies outside, not the thing itself. All outside things are themselves images cast into the mirror of nothingness. Things have no permanence or substantiality, despite the power of the Divine imagination to display them as integral parts of an entrancing dream. Human knowledge, then, is an internal image of an external image. To the extent that knowledge does in fact coincide with the reality of the known thing, with the entity fixed in the Divine knowledge, the internal image is more real than the external image. The external image, after all, pertains to the physical, inanimate realm of generation and corruption, but the internal image pertains to a higher level of existence and reality, a realm that is identical with life, awareness and consciousness.

The goal of realization is to gain knowledge of the essence of things and to act appropriately. The self must undergo a transformation such that it becomes indistinguishable from the infinity that it knows. True freedom is achieved only by those who pass beyond every specificity, and return to the original purity of the human self, known as *fitra*, or primordial nature.

Ibn 'Arabi's approach ends up in an admission of utter ignorance in the face of the Absolute. The ultimate, final knowledge is the knowledge of unknowingness, '*hayra*' or bewilderment. Ibn 'Arabi's grand contribution to Islamic learning was to loosen and unhinge all the fixed points of reference to which people attach themselves in their beliefs and opinions. The formula of Tawhid radically undermines everything other than Allah, including all beliefs and certainties concerning Allah and the world. Whatever fixed point of reference one seizes upon must be other than the Divine Himself, who is beyond all points of reference. Everything that appears as fixed and stable must be abandoned along with all things ephemeral and passing.

Death turns the self inside out. At death, our inner life becomes the outward configuration of His reality. The self is left to stand on its own without the stabilising fixity of the outside world. So-called objects disappear as independent things, and the Divine self-disclosure comes to the surface. We experience ourselves in forms appropriate to our own passions and aspirations.

We have lifted from you your covering, so your sight today is piercing.
—*Qur'an 50.22*

12 - The View of Love

You will not attain righteousness until you expend of what you love; and whatever thing you expend, Allah knows of it.
—Qur'an 3.92

Love is the energy-field that connects and unites the universe. It is the Power of the One Reality that interlinks all other temporary realities.
—Shaykh Fadhlalla Haeri

From all eternity the beloved unveiled his beauty in the solitude of the unseen;
He held up the mirror to his own face, he displayed his loveliness to himself.
He was both the spectator and the spectacle; no eye but his had surveyed the universe.
All was one, there was no duality, no pretence of 'mine' or 'thine'.
The vast orb of heaven, with its myriad of incomings and outgoings,
was concealed in a single point.
The creation lay cradled in the sleep of non-existence, like a child before it had breathed.
The eye of the beloved, seeing what was not, regarded nonentity as existent.
Although he beheld his attributes and qualities as a perfect whole in his own essence, yet he desired that they be displayed to him in another mirror, and that each one of his eternal attributes should become manifest accordingly in a diverse form. Therefore he created the verdant fields of time and space and

the life giving garden of the world, that every branch and leaf and fruit might show forth his various perfections.
The cypress gave a hint of his comely stature; the rose gave tidings of his beauteous countenance.
Wherever beauty peeped out, love appeared beside it; wherever beauty shone in a rosy cheek, love lit its torch from that flame. Wherever beauty dwelt in dark tresses, love came and found a heart entangled in their coils.
Beauty and love are as body and soul, beauty is the mine and love the precious stone. They have always been together from the very first; never have they travelled but in each other's company.
—Nuruddin Abdorahman Jami

This is love: to fly toward a secret sky,
to cause a hundred veils to fall each moment.
First, to let go of life.
In the end, to take a step without feet;
to regard this world as invisible,
and to disregard what appears to be the self.
Heart, I said, what a gift it has been
to enter this circle of lovers,
to see beyond seeing itself,
to reach and feel within the breast.
—Rumi

Yesterday at dawn, my friend said, How long will this unconsciousness go on?
You fill yourself with the sharp pain of love, rather than its fulfillment.
I said, 'But I can't get to you! You are the whole dark night, and I am a single candle.
My life is upside down because of you!'
The friend replied, I am your deepest being. Quit talking about wanting me!
I said, 'Then what is this restlessness?'
The friend: Does a drop stay still in the ocean?
Move with the entirety, and with the tiniest particular.

12 - The View of Love

Be the moisture in an oyster that helps to form one pearl.
—*Rumi*

None but God is loved in the existent things. It is He who is manifest within every beloved to the eye of every lover, and there is nothing in the existent realm that is not a lover.
—*Ibn 'Arabi*

The sincere lover is he who passes into the attributes of the Beloved, not he who pulls the Beloved down to his own level. He assumes as his own the traits of His names.
—*Ibn 'Arabi*

Alchemy

Love cannot be known in itself, but its attributes and names can be known and described. For Ibn 'Arabi, one of the most important of love's attributes has to do with the nature of its object. Whatever object it is that we love, it is always non-existent. We think that we love a real person or a real object, not a no-thingness. We love what we do not already have. We want to achieve something that we have not already achieved, or to be near to someone from whom we are far.

We assume we have gained the object person that we love but in fact the object still does not exist, because now love's object is the permanence of what was achieved, not the achievement itself. Permanence is an illusion, not an existing thing. When love sees the object, it is transferred to the permanence of that state whose existence it loves in that existent entity.

On its own, the Divine simply is, and on their own, the entities simply are not. But love is an attribute of the Divine, and love inherently strives for what is not. It expresses what is unexpressed, makes manifest what is hidden, and creates what has not been created. Love might be described as the innate tendency of Being to become manifest.

In and of themselves the entities remain fixed and immutable in non-existence. God loves to be known, so He loves the creatures through which He comes to be known. The objects of His love are by definition non-existent, and they will always remain non-existent, because His love for them is eternal. As long as there is love, one cannot conceive of the existence of the created thing along with it, so the created thing never comes into existence in truth.

The meaning of the name, Loving, *al-wadud*, is that the Divine constantly brings the universe into existence for the sake of His creatures. Although we are fixed entities and remain forever non-existent, the tongue of our own situation begs Allah to bestow existence upon us, and He responds by doing so. He is responding to Himself, for He is the tongue with which we speak. As all-comprehensive forms of being, human beings possess the attribute of love, and what they love remains forever non-existent. When the Divine and the universe are considered as two different realities, the object of human love may be the Divine, or someone or something in the universe. But when we understand that the universe is nothing but Divine self-disclosure, then we see that the object of love can be nothing but the Divine.

The object of love, however, is always non-existent, so the Divine stays forever non-existent in relation to His lovers as a separate other. In His essence He remains forever non-manifest, unknowable, and unattainable. Lovers and seekers strive to find Him, but the Divine who can be loved and sought is the Divine who can be conceptualised and understood. That is not the Divine in Himself, but rather the God of belief, the God that we understand, who is none other than the Divine as He shows Himself to us through His attributes.

The mark of archetypal human being love is his universal poverty, his utter annihilation of his egocentric self and his total focus on the infinite wealth of the Divine self-disclosure. Through a love for God that is absolute and unlimited, He loves all.

In love there is no two; there is no me or you. Love is empty of all attributes and activities that imply multiplicity.

12 - The View of Love

From each, Love demands a mystic silence.
What do all seek so earnestly? Tis Love.
Love is the subject of their inmost thoughts,
In Love no longer 'Thou' and 'I' exist,
For self has passed away in the Beloved.
Now will I draw aside the veil from Love,
And in the temple of mine inmost soul
Behold the Friend, Incomparable Love.
He who would know the secret of both worlds
Will find that the secret of them both is Love.
                                        —Attar

Whispering, then listening close, from the vision of one, casting away his all, instantly, out of an omnipotent hand.
Thus I read the knowledge of the scholars in a single word, and I reveal all the worlds to me with a simple glance.
I hear the many voices of those who pray in every tongue in a space of time shorter than a flash.
And I bring before me what before had been too far away to bear, in a blink of my eye.
I inhale the bouquet of gardens and the sweet scents clinging to the skirts of the four winds, in a simple breath.
I survey the far horizons round me in a momentary thought, and cross the seven heavens with a single step.
                                        —Ibn al-Farid

13 - *Alma Encantar*

Enduring the Tides of Time
Enduring the tides of time,
Abiding in love Divine,
Beauty speaks from eyes afar,
From silence love flows to depths unbound.

To Be
To hear the melody of the flowers in the wind.
To see the beauty of the Unseen.
To feel the tugs and pulls and urges of life.
To know when it is time to run, and time to rest;
time to laugh and time to cry;
time to hold on and time to let go.

Jahanara
Jahanara, the keeper of my hearts ring,
taken as I roam the starry desert nights.
Her radiance burns a thousand kindled suns,
Arjumand's palace lies in her shadow bleak.
A glance from her silences the roar of thunder,
Her pearly gown raises the breeze in its wake
Her breath causes the tree of life to spring forth,
A secret treasure is hidden in every sigh.
I have been awakened from my earthly dream by her scent,
To be taken back to the stillness of the place before I was born.

Oneness

Oneness of action is awareness of the source of action.
Oneness of attributes is awareness of the meaning behind all attributes.
Oneness of being is awareness of one's eternal Reality.
There is nothing to Give,
There is nothing to be Given.
There is no Birth,
There is no Death.
There is only Eternal Bliss,
Everything else is Divine Love.
May you come into yourself!

Glossary

accretion disk: gas orbiting around a black hole.

Advaita Vedanta: a school of Vedanta that posits that Brahman is the one and only Reality, even in the midst of apparent differences, that Reality is radically 'not-two' or 'non-dual'.

aham: the Sanskrit word for 'I'.

alchemy: the practice of transmuting substances, especially inexpensive substances (e.g., lead) into valuable substances (e.g., gold); many alchemical practices of medieval Europe survive in modern chemistry.

antimatter: a substance made of subatomic particles called antiparticles; an antiparticle (e.g., positron) has the same mass but the opposite electrical charge compared to its corresponding ordinary particle (e.g., electron).

appearance: the measurable total of all things present and knowable within the fabric of Pure Consciousness.

axiomatic: referring to self-evident absolute truths.

barzakh: a connecting link; something that is neither one thing nor the other, but allows for interrelationship between the two.

Big Bang theory: the present view of the beginning of creation in which the entire universe originated in an enormous explosion.

black hole: the result of a large collapsed star, an area from which even light cannot escape due to the strong gravity created by the black hole's extreme mass.

bootstrap: level that is both elementary and composite, made out of particles of the same kind; each time they are divided, they produce the same kind of particles.

Bose-Einstein condensate: a special state condensed phase in which the many parts initially behave as a whole, but then become whole.

centrifugal: moving away from the center or axis.

centripetal: moving toward the center or axis.

completeness principle: the physicists' ultimate goal of having a unified theory of all physics.

consciousness: sense of existence, or awareness of simply being; the fabric of reality; the medium from which every aspect of our experience manifests.

Copenhagen interpretation: interpretation of the quantum theory that rejected determinism, accepting instead the statistical nature of reality, and rejected objectivity, accepting instead that material reality depends in part on how we choose to observe it.

cosmos: the totality of human experience, interior and exterior, individual and collective.

dogma: a primary belief or set of beliefs held to be true, upon which an ideology is based; such beliefs cannot be challenged because they form the foundation of the ideology.

Doppler shift: a galaxy that is moving away from us at high speed has its spectral lines of light shifted to the red in proportion to its speed; this discovery aided our understanding that the universe is expanding.

Glossary

ego: the limited or false self; contrast with true self.

empirical science: science based on evidence.

energy: the potential to do work, or create change.

entropy: a measure of how disorganised, random-like in appearance, a physical system is; also an emergent macroscopic property.

erg: a unit of energy.

event horizon: the boundary containing the material of a collapsed star.

eye of certainty: in Sufism, the second attainment in the way of illumination, the spiritual methods and practices contained within the body of Sufism.

fitra: the original purity of the human self, or primordial nature.

gauge symmetry: regarding field transformations, if gauge symmetry remains exact, the associated fields remain completely hidden or trapped inside other quanta; if gauge symmetry is broken, different components of the gauge field can manifest themselves very differently.

gluons: quantum particles that mediate the interactions of quarks and leptons.

Gnostic: referring to gnosis, a Greek word meaning 'knowledge'; within the world's spiritual traditions, gnosis means a particular kind of spiritual knowledge or insight.

hadrons: particles made of quarks; because the number of possible hadrons is infinite, they represent a new, endless level of reality.

hayra: the ultimate, final knowledge, the knowledge of unknowingness, or bewilderment.

hierarchy of the Cosmos: a model of a ranking of orders of events according to their to their holistic capacity; what is whole at one stage becomes a part of a larger whole at the next stage.

holon: that which is simultaneously both whole and part.

hypothesis: a supposition; an idea that is 'put under' our reasoning, as a provisional base, which is to be tested experimentally for its truth or falsity.

Idea: in Plato's philosophy, an Idea (or 'Form') is an eternal, unchanging, perfect entity, beyond space and time; an Idea serves as the basis for an impermanent, changing, imperfect entity that exists in space and time; all imperfect objects in space and time have a corresponding perfect Idea; the highest Idea is the Idea of the Good.

imaginal (or thought) experiments: tests of hypotheses that take place in the imagination because they cannot be performed in the laboratory or the 'real world'.

imaginal knowledge: our views about who we are and our place in the universe, or, more correctly, the universe's place within us.

I-ness: the deeper identity; the true self.

interspace: the location of human beings, the 'middle people', between what seems tangible and what is beyond.

invariance: the principle that there are things that don't change.

irrational number: a real number that cannot be written as the ratio of two integers; such a number is a non-repeating decimal. The square root of 2 ($\sqrt{2}$) is an irrational number, as is 'pi', π.

Kelvin: a unit of temperature measurement; 0 degrees Kelvin in absolute zero, the coldest temperature possible.

knowledge of certainty: in Sufism, the first attainment in the way of illumination, gained from knowing the doctrine of the spiritual path; this forms the body or container of Sufism.

law of entropy increase: the entropy within any closed system will always increase.

light: often the preferred model of spiritual traditions to describe consciousness; light transcends the world of space and time, it is self-evident, and everything else is simply infinite shadows pointing back as signs and metaphors to that original light.

Lights of Consciousness: both the outer cosmos as explored by modern empirical science and spirituality and the inner dimension of the human psyche; dimensions or views arising in and from consciousness.

local causality: distant events cannot instantaneously influence local objects without mediation.

logos: the ruling principle of nature.

maya: (Sanskrit) an illusion, a false perception of the world; a delusion, a false belief about the world.

metaphor: a way in which we relate to the world and ourselves; not to be mistaken for true reality.

metaphysics: the branch of philosophy that seeks to determine what 'being' is, what exists, and how existence is structured; Aristotle's philosophy of being and existence is described in his text, entitled Metaphysics.

models: images of the material world made to render it comprehensible and as simple as possible.

natural philosophy: the term used to described the study of the natural world; since the nineteenth century replaced largely by the term 'science'.

neutron star: remnant of a supernova.

noumenon: that which is; the thing-in-itself, contrasted with that which appears to be (the phenomenon).

ontology: the philosophy of being, concerned with the ultimate nature of existence.

perfect symmetry: equal amounts of matter and antimatter, which always form pure energy; state of the universe before the Big Bang.

phenomenon: that which appears to be; how reality appears to our senses, contrasted with how reality really is (the noumenon).

philosophy: the study of general and fundamental problems, such as those connected with existence, knowledge, values, reason, mind and language.

photon: a single quantum of light.

pion: the 'glue' that holds together the protons and neutrons in the nucleus.

pulsar: a rotating neutron star.

pumped system: a system of vibrating electrically charged molecules in cell walls into which energy is pumped.

Pure Consciousness: the nature of reality that exists at every level; the one Truth; the absolute certainty of our existence; the essence of everything we know.

prophet: someone who lives in deepest relationship with Pure Consciousness and reveals to others the way to live that relationship.

quantum electromechanics: the theory of the interactions of electrons with light.

quantum: a discrete unit of matter or action.

quarks: particles that make up a hadron; there are three types, or 'flavors': up, down, strange, charm, bottom and top.

quasar: an extremely bright region in the center of a galaxy; the energy emitted by a quasar originates from mass falling into the accretion disk surrounding a supermassive black hole.

rational number: a real number that can be written as a the ratio of two integers; such a number may be an integer, a finite decimal, or a repeating decimal.

real number: a number that can be located on an infinitely long number line that stretches from negative infinity to positive infinity.

red giant: an aging star that has begun to exhaust its hydrogen supply and is nearing the end of its life.

red shift: shift in the light from distant galaxies that is proportional to their distance from us; this discovery aided our understanding that the universe is expanding.

sage: one who is exclusively devoted to realizing the Transcendental Reality.

science: the search for the truth of the physical world (outer/object); a path to gaining reliable knowledge through careful observation and testing.

scientific model: a mental, metaphysical image; a mathematical representation of what we 'think' something is; a metaphor by which we relate to the world and ourselves.

seer: one who sees, especially one who sees and experiences realms other than the material or physical.

singularity: a point where a property such as mass is infinite.

soul: the unconditioned essential reality within.

space-time: when observed, space-time appears as a certain amount of space and a certain amount of time; however, the amount of which is perceived as space and the amount of which is perceived as time are not fixed; they are dependent upon the motion of the observer.

spiritual heart: in Sufism, the instrument of intuition.

spiritual science: search for understanding using the technology of introspection and intuitions energised by 'Divine' attributes of will, knowledge, and love to probe the complex layers of the self with the aim of revealing the underlying meaning behind the forms manifesting as thoughts, feelings and dreams.

spirituality: the search for the truth in the nature of consciousness (inner/subject).

spontaneous broken symmetry: asymmetrical solutions to symmetrical equations.

standard models: models that describe the world from the subatomic scale, which is the domain of quantum physics, to the large-scale description of the cosmos, which is the domain of general relativity.

subject–object distinction: recognition of a separation of the 'out there' from the 'in here'.

supernova: a violent explosion that results from the collapse of a large star that has exhausted its energy supply.

symmetry: the organising principle in quantum physics.

synchronicity: the psychological phenomena of attributing a pattern to different random events, an impulse to seek meaning to existence.

theory: a form of insight, a way of looking at the world, and not a form of knowledge of how the world is.

transcend: when a holon has emergent or novel creative properties that are not merely the sum of its parts; new levels of organisation come into being that cannot be reduced to the previous dimension.

transcendental number: an irrational number that is not the root of any polynomial equation. The number π is both irrational and transcendental, as is Euler's number, e.

translational invariance: motion of an object without seeing the difference and without changing its state.

transpersonal: that which is beyond the person or individual self

true self: the essence of consciousness; although our thoughts, feelings, and personality may vary considerably, the essence of consciousness remains the same.

truth of certainty: in Sufism, the third attainment in the way of illumination, the knowledge that illuminates.

unity: all manifestation arises from a prior and inherently indivisible unity; everything that appears is developed from what is already there, inherently and potentially.

universal prototype or archetype: in Sufism, symbolises four aspects of Divine manifestation; the archetype is the 'uncreated', pre-existent aspect within things. In the move toward creation it is the first articulation of the One, the first to contain objectivity. The archetype is also light, as well as the active agent in the prototypical human form. It is the Divine's own image, the centre of the universe and the spirit of the Absolute. It is the word made manifest.

universality and simplicity principle: the same laws governing the motion of the stars also apply to the motion of objects on Earth.

upadhi: a Sanskrit word meaning 'condition', attribute', 'limitation'.

vacuum fluctuation: when a particle and its anti-particle spring into virtual existence at a point in space and then immediately annihilate each other.

vacuum polarisation: an effect, taking place in the space between an atomic nucleus and an orbiting electron, that slightly changes the orbit of the electron.

Vedanta: a Hindu philosophical system that presents the ultimate interpretation of the Vedas, the primary Hindu scriptures.

virtual quantum: a quantum that comes into existence in empty space and quickly disappears.

way of illumination: in Sufism, consists of three attainments:

the knowledge of certainty, the eye of certainty and the truth of certainty.

white dwarf: a small star that has exhausted its energy supply and collapsed.

Zen: a tradition within Buddhism that emphasizes meditation, the experience of insight, and the direct expression of one's true nature.

About the Author

Born in Basra Iraq from a family of scholars, Adnan was schooled in Scotland in his early years. He spent his teenage years in Kuwait where he finished his undergraduate studies. He returned to Scotland for further study, full time research and work. This is where his spiritual journey and seeking began although his quest for deeper understanding was evident throughout his life. He now lives in Belgium with his wife and four children.

He works in the field of Electronic Engineering, Instrumentation Engineering and Telecommunications Engineering and holds a PhD in Electronics Engineering from the University of Strathclyde. He is also an IEEE Senior Member. Adnan has also released several publications and published patents in the field of digital signal processing related to electronic communications and measurement sciences.

He is a frequent speaker at many international Sufi conferences and gatherings held in South Africa and in Europe and is a respected scholar and researcher in both his field of scientific study as well as spirituality and the Qur'an.

www.ingramcontent.com/pod-product-compliance
Lightning Source LLC
Chambersburg PA
CBHW021404290426
44108CB00010B/373